ACCA
and
FIA

ACCA Business and Technology
(RQF Level 4)

Business and Technology (BT)

EXAM KIT

KAPLAN
PUBLISHING

British Library Cataloguing-in-Publication Data

A catalogue record for this book is available from the British Library.

Published by:

Kaplan Publishing UK

179 – 191 Borough High Street

London

SE1 1HR

ISBN: 978-1-83735-271-5

Printed and bound in Great Britain

CONTENTS

You will find a wealth of other resources to help you with your studies on the following sites: www.Mykaplan.co.uk and www.**acca**global.com/students/

Quality and accuracy are of the utmost importance to us so if you spot an error in any of our products, please send an email to mykaplanreporting@kaplan.com with full details.

Our Quality Co-ordinator will work with our technical team to verify the error and take action to ensure it is corrected in future editions.

INDEX TO OBJECTIVE TEST QUESTIONS AND ANSWERS

PRACTICE QUESTIONS

INDEX TO MULTI-TASK QUESTIONS AND ANSWERS

PRACTICE QUESTIONS

EXAM TECHNIQUE

- **Do not skip any of the material** in the syllabus.
- **Read each question** *very* carefully.
- **Double-check your answer** before committing yourself to it.
- Answer **every** question – if you do not know an answer, you don't lose anything by guessing. Think carefully before you **guess**.
- If you are answering a multiple-choice question, **eliminate first those answers that you know are wrong**. Then choose the most appropriate answer from those that are left.
- **Don't panic** if you realise you've answered a question incorrectly. Getting one question wrong will not mean the difference between passing and failing

Computer-based exams – tips

- Do not attempt a CBE until you have **completed all study material** relating to it.
- On the ACCA website there is a CBE demonstration. It is **ESSENTIAL** that you attempt this before your real CBE. You will become familiar with how to move around the CBE screens and the way that questions are formatted, increasing your confidence and speed in the actual exam.
- Be sure you understand how to use the **software** before you start the exam. If in doubt, ask the assessment centre staff to explain it to you.
- Questions are **displayed on the screen** and answers are entered using keyboard and mouse. At the end of the exam, you are given a certificate showing the result you have achieved.
- The CBE question types are as follows:
  - Multiple choice – where you are required to choose one answer from a list of options provided by clicking on the appropriate 'radio button'
  - Multiple response – where you are required to select more than one response from the options provided by clicking on the appropriate tick boxes (typically choose two options from the available list)
  - Multiple response matching – where you are required to indicate a response to a number of related statements by clicking on the 'radio button' which corresponds to the appropriate response for each statement
  - Number entry – where you are required to key in a response to a question shown on the screen.
- Note that the CBE variant of the examination will not require you to input text, although you may be required to choose the correct text from options available.
- You need to be sure you **know how to answer questions** of this type before you sit the exam, through practice.

EXAM-SPECIFIC INFORMATION

THE EXAM

FORMAT OF THE COMPUTER-BASED EXAM

	Number of marks
30 compulsory objective test questions (2 marks each)	60
16 compulsory objective test questions (1 mark each)	16
6 compulsory multi-task questions (4 marks each)	24
Total time allowed: 2 hours	100

- In any exam there will be roughly 8 or 9 questions for **each** of the six main syllabus areas
- Two mark questions will usually comprise the following answer types:
  (i) Multiple choice with four options (A, B, C or D)
  (ii) Ask you to select two correct answers from a choice of four
- One mark questions will usually comprise the following answer types:
  (i) Multiple choice with two options (A or B)
  (ii) Ask you to select whether a statement is true or false
- Each four mark multi-task question will be split into two or more parts. They can involve any of the above answer types as well as selection of multiple responses from a list. Expect to see one multi-task question on each section of the syllabus.
- ACCA official statistics have shown that most students do not find the exam time pressured

PASS MARK

The pass mark for all ACCA Qualification examinations is 50%.

DETAILED SYLLABUS, STUDY GUIDE AND CBE SPECIMEN EXAM

The detailed syllabus and study guide written by the ACCA, along with the specimen exam, can be found at:

accaglobal.com/business-and-technology

ACCA SUPPORT

For additional support with your studies please also refer to the ACCA Global website.

KAPLAN'S RECOMMENDED REVISION APPROACH

QUESTION PRACTICE IS THE KEY TO SUCCESS

Success in professional examinations relies upon you acquiring a firm grasp of the required knowledge at the tuition phase. In order to be able to do the questions, knowledge is essential.

However, the difference between success and failure often hinges on your exam technique on the day and making the most of the revision phase of your studies.

The **Kaplan study text** is the starting point, designed to provide the underpinning knowledge to tackle all questions. However, in the revision phase, pouring over text books is not the answer.

Kaplan Online progress tests help you consolidate your knowledge and understanding and are a useful tool to check whether you can remember key topic areas.

Kaplan pocket notes are designed to help you quickly revise a topic area, however you then need to practice questions. There is a need to progress to full exam standard questions as soon as possible, and to tie your exam technique and technical knowledge together.

The importance of question practice cannot be over-emphasised.

The recommended approach below is designed by expert tutors in the field, in conjunction with their knowledge of the examiner.

The approach taken for the fundamental exams is to revise by topic area.

You need to practice as many questions as possible in the time you have left.

OUR AIM

Our aim is to get you to the stage where you can attempt exam standard questions confidently, to time, in a closed book environment, with no supplementary help (i.e. to simulate the real examination experience).

Practising your exam technique on real past examination questions, in timed conditions, is also vitally important for you to assess your progress and identify areas of weakness that may need more attention in the final run up to the examination.

The approach below shows you which questions you should use to build up to coping with exam standard question practice, and references to the sources of information available should you need to revisit a topic area in more detail.

Remember that in the real examination, all you have to do is:

- attempt all questions required by the exam
- only spend the allotted time on each question, and
- get at least 50% right!

Try and practice this approach on every question you attempt from now to the real exam.

THE KAPLAN BUSINESS AND TECHNOLOGY REVISION PLAN

Stage 1: Assess areas of strengths and weaknesses

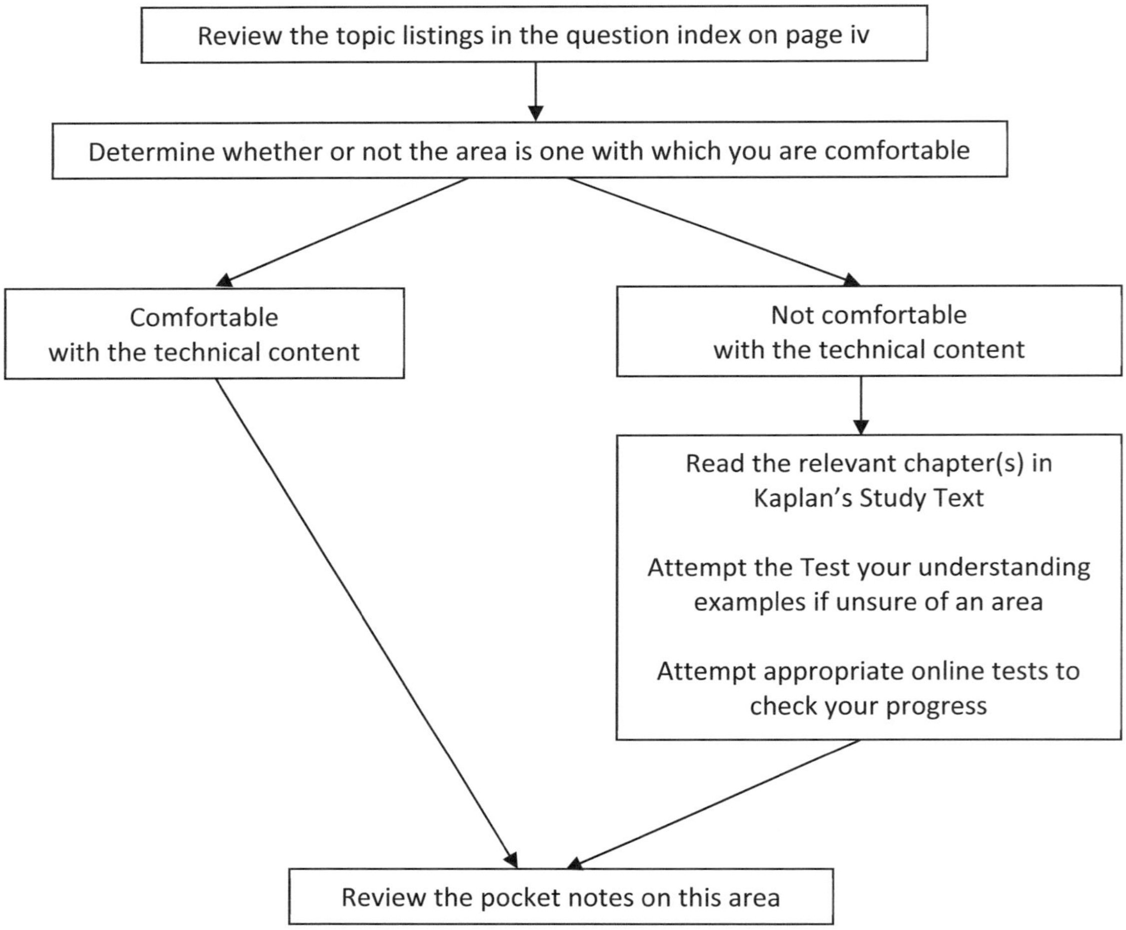

Stage 2: Practice questions

Ensure that you revise all syllabus areas as questions could be asked on anything.

Try to avoid referring to text books and notes and the model answer until you have completed your attempt.

Try to answer the question in the allotted time.

Review your attempt with the model answer. If you got the answer wrong, can you see why? Was the problem a lack of knowledge or a failure to understand the question fully?

Decide on your best course of action using the boxes below.

Comfortable with question attempt

Only revisit when comfortable with questions on all topic areas

Not comfortable with question attempts

Focus on these areas by:

- Reworking test your understanding examples in Kaplan's Study Text
- Revisiting the technical content from Kaplan's pocket notes
- Working any remaining questions on that area in the exam kit

Stage 3: Final pre-exam revision

We recommend that you **attempt at least one two hour mock examination** containing a set of previously unseen exam standard questions.

It is important that you get a feel for the breadth of coverage of a real exam without advanced knowledge of the topic areas covered – just as you will expect to see on the real exam day.

Ideally this mock should be sat in timed, closed book, real exam conditions and could be:

- a mock examination offered by your tuition provider, and/or
- the specimen exam in the back of this exam kit.

Section 1

OBJECTIVE TEST QUESTIONS – SECTION A

THE BUSINESS ORGANISATION

1 **Which of the following is NOT a key feature of an organisation?**

A Controlled performance

B Collective goals

C Social arrangements

D Creation of a product or service **(2 marks)**

2 **Are the following statements true or false?**

Statement	**True**	**False**
Private companies can raise share capital by advertising to the general public.		
Private companies can raise share capital from venture capitalists		

(2 marks)

3 **The public sector is normally concerned with which of the following activities?**

A Making profit from the sale of goods

B Providing services to specific groups funded from charitable donations

C The provision of basic government services

D Raising funds by subscriptions from members to provide common services **(2 marks)**

4 **A Co is a company which specialises in forestry. It has recently purchased B Co, which runs a chain of recreational resorts. A has allowed B to build several new resorts on land which is owned by A, but which it is no longer able to use. The resorts have proven highly profitable and popular. Which of the following best explains the reason for the improved performance of the combined entity?**

A Specialisation

B Social interactivity

C Synergy

D Service **(2 marks)**

5 **Which of the following statements regarding limited companies is correct?**

A Public limited companies have access to a wider pool of finance than partnerships or sole traders

B Both public and private limited companies are allowed to sell shares to the public

C Companies are always owned by many different investors

D Shareholders are liable for any debts the company may incur **(2 marks)**

6 Consider the following list of different organisations:

(i) Government departments

(ii) Partnerships

(iii) Charities

(iv) Companies

Which of these organisations would normally be classified as BOTH a not-for-profit organisation AND a private sector organisation?

A (i) and (iii) only

B (iii) only

C (i) only

D (ii) and (iii) only **(2 marks)**

7 'An organisation that is owned and democratically controlled by its members.'

To which type of organisation does this definition relate?

A Charities

B Non-governmental organisations

C Co-operatives

D Private limited companies **(2 marks)**

8 Westeros is an organisation which imports computers into country A and sells them to the public in order to make a profit. It is owned by fifteen individual investors, each of whom owns an equal number of shares in Westeros. Westeros is not a public limited company.

Which of the following is likely to be the most appropriate source of finance for Westeros?

A Central government funding

B The existing owners of Westeros

C Issue of shares to the public

D Donations from the public **(2 marks)**

9 **Are the following statements true or false?**

Statement	**True**	**False**
Not-for-profit organisations (NFPs) have varied objectives, which depend on the needs of their members or the sections of society they were created to benefit.		
The primary objective of government-funded organisations is to reduce costs of their operations and thus minimise the burden on tax payers.		

(2 marks)

10 **Which of the following statements is true?**

A Limited company status means that a company is only allowed to trade up to a predetermined turnover level in any one year

B For organisations that have limited company status, ownership and control are legally separate **(1 mark)**

BUSINESS ORGANISATION AND STRUCTURE

11 **Which of the following statements regarding the entrepreneurial structure is correct?**

A It usually allows for defined career paths for employees

B It often enjoys strong goal congruence throughout the organisation

C It can normally cope with significant diversification and growth **(1 mark)**

12 **Which of the following statements about an organisational chart is true?**

A An organisational chart outlines the organisation's financial performance

B An organisational chart displays the formal structure and reporting relationships with the organisation

C An organisational chart tracks the organisation's sales and marketing strategies

D An organisational chart provides a detailed list of the companies' employees and their qualifications **(2 marks)**

13 H Co makes a variety of unrelated products, including bicycles, furniture and electronics. It is aware that each of these products requires very different strategies and functions. H wishes to use a structure that will allow for each product to be managed separately, but wishes to minimise its overall administrative costs.

Which of the following organisational structures would be most appropriate for H Co to adopt?

A Divisional

B Entrepreneurial

C Functional

D Matrix **(2 marks)**

14 **Which of the following structures results in a potential loss of control over key operating decisions and a reduction in goal congruence?**

A Matrix

B Entrepreneurial

C Functional

D Geographic **(2 marks)**

15 **Are the following statements true or false?**

Statement	**True**	**False**
Tall organisations typically have narrow spans of control.		
A 'flat' organisation is one that has a short scalar chain.		

(2 marks)

16 Consider the following benefits:

(i) Reduced training costs within the organisation

(ii) Better local decisions due to local expertise

(iii) Better motivation of staff

(iv) Reduction in suboptimal behaviour

Which of these are advantages of the centralisation of decision-making within an organisation?

A (i) and (ii) only

B (i), (ii) and (iii) only

C (iii) only

D (i) and (iv) only **(2 marks)**

17 Sansa Co is planning to outsource all of its functions to third party suppliers – even those that it feels are core activities which give the company competitive advantage in the market place.

Which boundaryless structure is Sansa planning to adopt?

A Virtual

B Hollow **(1 mark)**

18 Sandra manufactures motor vehicles. She has recently decided to stop the manufacturing of car windows and, instead, will buy the windows ready-made from an external supplier. The remaining components of the motor vehicles will continue to be made by Sandra.

Which of the following structural concepts does Sandra's plan most closely match?

A Virtual organisation

B Shared service agreement

C Matrix structure

D Modular structure **(2 marks)**

19 Offshoring refers to the transfer of existing staff members to other countries with lower wage rates.

Is this statement TRUE or FALSE?

A True

B False **(1 mark)**

20 Adopting a shared services approach refers to the centralisation of an internal service within the organisation. The operations of the internal service will be unaffected.

Is this statement TRUE or FALSE?

A True

B False **(1 mark)**

21 Stark Limited is a company that currently manufactures metal tubing. It has recently decided to open a series of new manufacturing plants within country H which it believes will help it to break into the European market.

Which level of strategy planning would this decision relate to?

A Functional

B Strategic

C Tactical

D Operational **(2 marks)**

22 According to Anthony's hierarchy, there are three levels of planning within an organisation. Which level of planning is usually undertaken by the organisation's junior management?

A Operational

B Tactical

C Strategic

D Applied **(2 marks)**

23 When considering the roles of different departments, which one of the following is likely to be concerned with identifying and satisfying customer needs?

A Production

B Research and development

C Marketing

D Purchasing **(2 marks)**

24 An online retailer using the 4Ps marketing mix model should categorise its website under the category of 'place'.

Is this statement TRUE or FALSE?

A True

B False **(1 mark)**

25 A company with a marketing orientation believes that:

A products should be sold actively and aggressively

B meeting customer needs better than competitors is the key to corporate success

C the level of sales, advertising and sales promotion is key to corporate success

D producing goods and services of optimum quality is the key to corporate success **(2 marks)**

26 The use of basic rather than the extended marketing mix is more appropriate when a company:

A directly interacts with consumers, such as a supermarket

B specialises in the manufacturing of computer components that are then sold on to an intermediary

C provides services such as telecommunications

D aims to minimise its expenditure on marketing **(2 marks)**

27 Which of the following is NOT part of the marketing mix?

A People

B Promotion

C Physical evidence

D Public relations **(2 marks)**

28 **What element of the marketing mix are the following situations concerned with?**

Situation	Product	Place
Arryn Co manufactures and sells board games. It is currently considering the packaging, quality and design of the board games as part of a strategic review.		
A key decision when reviewing the marketing mix is whether to sell directly to the consumer or indirectly through an intermediary.		

(2 marks)

29 **A business is planning to launch a new product. It plans to sell this product in Europe and America, but will charge more in America as it feels American customers will be willing to pay more. What type of pricing strategy is the business considering?**

A Penetration pricing

B Going rate pricing

C Price skimming

D Price discrimination **(2 marks)**

30 **Printers are available to buy very cheaply. However the cartridges required to operate them are expensive. What kind of pricing strategy are the printer manufacturers using?**

A Price penetration

B Price skimming

C Captive product pricing

D 'Going rate' pricing **(2 marks)**

31 **At which stage of the strategic marketing process will the organisation have to segment its market?**

A Analysis

B Review

C Implementation

D Choice **(2 marks)**

32 Promotion is about encouraging customers to buy the organisation's products or services by moving them through four stages:

(i) Action

(ii) Awareness

(iii) Desire

(iv) Interest

What is the correct order for these four stages?

A (ii), (iv), (iii), (i)

B (i), (iv), (iii), (ii)

C (iv), (ii), (iii), (i)

D (ii), (iii), (iv), (i) **(2 marks)**

ORGANISATIONAL CULTURE IN BUSINESS

33 Are the following statements true or false?

Statement	**True**	**False**
Culture was expressed by Handy as 'the sum of the belief, knowledge, attitudes, norms and customs that prevail in an organisation'.		
The tales of company creation, such as difficulties the founder had to face and how they managed to overcome them successfully often form a part of organisational culture.		

(2 marks)

34 John begins a new job at a company. He discovers that, unlike his previous job, all staff members dress casually. According to Schein, which level of culture is John observing?

A Artefacts

B Espoused values

C Informal rules

D Basic assumptions **(2 marks)**

35 The first leaders of the organisation tend to define its later culture.

Which major writer on culture came to this conclusion?

A Handy

B Schein **(1 mark)**

36 Which of the following is one of the three levels of culture described by Schein?

A Things that are short term only, such as staffing levels

B Things that are difficult to identify as they are unseen and often unconscious

C Things that endure, such as organisational hierarchy

D Things that initially appear superficial, such as timekeeping rules **(2 marks)**

37 **Which TWO of the following are cultural types identified by Handy?**

(i) Role

(ii) Person

(iii) Bureaucratic

(iv) Individual

A (ii) and (iii) only

B (i) and (iii) only

C (i), (ii) and (iii) only

D (i) and (ii) only **(2 marks)**

38 The informal organisation can either enhance or hold the business back.

Is this statement TRUE or FALSE?

A True

B False **(1 mark)**

39 **According to Handy's theory, in the person culture which of the following would be correct?**

A Contribution made by each employee is recognised and appreciated

B Status symbols are there to remind staff of their place

C People believe that if they meet their job requirement, they will slowly progress to the senior management

D Rules are put in place and must be strictly followed by all **(2 marks)**

40 **Which of the four cultural types popularised by Handy is often found in organisations with an entrepreneurial structure?**

A Task

B Person

C Power

D Role **(2 marks)**

41 Research has indicated that workers in country A display characteristics such as the desire for material wealth and possessions, while workers in country B value personal relationships, belonging and the quality of life.

According to Hofstede's theory, these distinctions relate to which of the following cultural dimensions?

A Motivation towards achievement and success

B Power-distance

C Indulgence-restraint

D Uncertainty avoidance **(2 marks)**

42 Consider the following cultural 'dimensions' as popularised by Hofstede.

(i) High uncertainty avoidance

(ii) High motivation towards achievement and success

(iii) Low power distance

(iv) Individualism

In country A, most businesses are highly bureaucratic with many defined rules for employees. However, even junior staff members are usually involved in the creation of these rules, as they expect to have a say in the running of the business.

Which TWO of the cultural dimensions identified above are shown to exist in country A?

A (i) and (ii)

B (i) and (iii)

C (ii) and (iii)

D (iii) and (iv) **(2 marks)**

43 'The ____________ is the network of relationships that exist within an organisation and arises through common interests and friendships between members of staff.'

Which word fits the gap in the above definition?

grapevine/scalar chain/ informal organisation*

*delete as appropriate **(1 mark)**

44 GHF Co is currently examining its organisational structure, with particular focus on its informal organisation.

Which of the following statements regarding the informal organisation is correct?

A If managers become involved in the informal organisation, employee motivation and productivity usually fall

B The informal organisation typically tends to encourage employees to act as individuals

C The informal organisation may form a significant part of the opposition managers face if they attempt to implement changes in the organisation

D Interdivisional communication tends to be weaker through the informal network when compared with formal communications **(2 marks)**

INFORMATION TECHNOLOGY AND INFORMATION SYSTEMS IN BUSINESS

45 **Are the following statements true or false?**

Statement	True	False
Big data contains both financial and non-financial data.		
Cloud computing allows storage and accessing of data programs over the internet instead of on the computer's hard drive.		

(2 marks)

46 Are the following statements true or false?

Statement	**True**	**False**
A spreadsheet can perform the task of presenting numerical data in the form of graphs and charts.		
A spreadsheet can perform the task of applying 'What if?' scenarios.		

(2 marks)

47 U Co has recently commissioned a report into the potential sales of a prototype product that it has developed. The report is extremely detailed and filled with jargon. The management of U are finding it difficult to follow the report's findings.

Which of the following criteria of good quality information is NOT being met by this report?

A Relevant

B Complete

C Accurate

D Understandable **(2 marks)**

48 Which of the following is a reasonable drawback of using a database?

A It is difficult for two people to use it at the same time

B The quantity of information is limited to just a few thousand records

C Set up and maintenance costs can outweigh the benefits of using it **(1 mark)**

49 Which of the following systems pools data from internal and external sources and makes information available to senior managers for strategic, unstructured decision-making?

A Expert Systems (ES)

B Decision Support Systems (DSS)

C Executive Information Systems (EIS)

D Transaction Processing Systems (TPS) **(2 marks)**

50 Are the following statements true or false?

Statement	**True**	**False**
Blockchain technology presents the possibility of an accounting system that can be continuously updated and verified without the threat of being altered or corrupted.		
Phishing is a type of computer virus.		

(2 marks)

51 Which of the following systems is being described?

	Decision support system	Expert system	Management information system
This system type converts data from a transaction processing system into information for monitoring performance and maintaining co-ordination.			
When the government authority at the end of the tax year sends thousands of notifications to people with an estimate of the tax they need to pay, these letters are likely to be produced by this system type.			

(2 marks)

52 FFK company is a small manufacturing company supplying wholesale customers who order goods by phone. It operates from one site and has its own internal accounts department. Labels for goods to be despatched are printed on-site and the goods are then collected by a local courier service for delivery. Inventory levels for key components are monitored electronically and suppliers receive automatic notification when deliveries are required.

Based on the information provided, which ONE of the following features of FFK company's business model are MOST likely to expose them to cyber-security threats?

A Orders placed by phone

B Internal accounts department

C Use of a local courier service

D Inventory arrangement with component suppliers **(2 marks)**

53 Which of the following is NOT a benefit of big data analytics

A Improved decision making

B Greater focus on customer needs and wants

C Increased security of data

D Product innovation **(2 marks)**

54 Which TWO of the following statements about the impact of technological developments on the role of accountants are true?

A Automation and artificial intelligence allow the accountant to focus their time on verifying low level transactions

B Distributed ledger technology increases the need for auditors to audit all transactions

C Cloud accounting allows accountants to work collaboratively together and with their clients

D Big data and data analytics assist auditors to target key business risks **(2 marks)**

STAKEHOLDERS

55 Employees are ______ stakeholders, while finance providers are _______ stakeholders.

Which two words fill the gaps in the above sentence?

A Internal, Connected

B External, Internal

C Connected, Outsiders

D Internal, Suppliers **(2 marks)**

56 Stakeholders can be classified in several different ways, including:

(i) Primary

(ii) External

(iii) Connected

(iv) Secondary

Which TWO categories would pressure groups usually be included within?

A (i) and (iii)

B (i) and (iv)

C (ii) and (iv) **(1 mark)**

57 **A is a large company whose shares are owned by a large number of individual investors, who do not wish to engage with the company's decision making despite having full rights to do so. When using Mendelow's matrix this stakeholder group would be classed as:**

A minimal effort

B keep informed

C keep satisfied

D key players **(2 marks)**

58 A company is using a communication strategy aimed at explaining the rationale behind its actions to its stakeholders. Using Mendelow's matrix, these stakeholders would be categorised as 'minimal effort'.

Is this statement TRUE or FALSE?

A True

B False **(1 mark)**

59 The interests of customers and shareholders can often appear to conflict – for example in the quality of goods and services.

Is this statement TRUE or FALSE?

A True

B False **(1 mark)**

60 According to Mendelow, which of the following is an appropriate approach to take towards stakeholders who have low levels of power and low levels of interest?

A minimal effort

B keep informed

C keep satisfied

D key players **(2 marks)**

EXTERNAL ANALYSIS – POLITICAL AND LEGAL FACTORS

61 Which of the following would a transport company monitor under the Political heading as part of a PEST analysis?

A Tracking systems to monitor driver hours/anti-theft devices/developments in tyre technology

B State of the economy/oil price movements/a rise in interest rates

C Fuel tax/congestion charges in cities/plans to build new roads

D Predicted car numbers and usage/public concerns over safety **(2 marks)**

62 Consider the following statements:

1 A political system can be defined as 'a complete set of institutions, political organisations and interest groups, the relationship between those institutions and the political rules and norms that govern their functions.'

2 Nationalisation of an industry often involves government selling some of its assets in a bid to promote competition.

Which of these statements is/are correct?

A 1 only

B 2 only

C Both

D Neither **(2 marks)**

63 Supra-national sources of legal authority include:

A United Nations resolutions

B US legislation

C UK Government legislation

D UK High Court decisions **(2 marks)**

64 Data Protection legislation, such as The Data Protection Act in the UK, typically focuses on:

A issues concerning data held about incorporated entities

B rights of the individual with regards to withholding information about oneself

C the way data about the individual is to be obtained, used and stored

D aligning the information requirements between different countries **(2 marks)**

65 Which of the following are typical rights of individuals with respect to data stored about them in data protection legislation?

	Yes	**No**
Right of subject access – individuals are entitled to be told whether the data controller holds personal data about them.		
Right to prevent processing for the purposes of direct marketing.		

(2 marks)

66 Consider the following two scenarios.

(i) Alex wants to request his personal credit report from a credit file company for free, using typical data protection legislation.

(ii) Alex receives a large amount of unsolicited (junk) mail. Using the data protection act, he wishes to have these marketing activities blocked.

In which of these scenarios would typical data protection legislation support Alex?

A (i) only

B (ii) only

C Both

D Neither **(2 marks)**

EXTERNAL ANALYSIS – ECONOMIC FACTORS

67 Consider the following statements:

1 The equilibrium point of demand and supply curves represents the price at which all goods produced are purchased, with no surplus or shortage in the market.

2 As the selling price of a product increases, the number of units supplied by the market will also tend to rise.

Which of these statements is/are correct?

A 1 only

B 2 only

C Both

D Neither **(2 marks)**

68 In the short term, the average cost per unit of a product rises because the total fixed costs are spread over a greater number of units of output.

Is this statement TRUE or FALSE?

A True

B False **(1 mark)**

69 A shift in the demand curve for a product is caused by changes in the conditions of demand, rather than a change in the price of the product.

Is this statement TRUE or FALSE?

A True

B False **(1 mark)**

70 **G Co increases the selling price of its only product, the GF1000 by 5%. This causes a reduction in the number of units it sells by 8%. Is the GF1000's price elasticity of demand likely to be:**

A Less than 1

B Equal to 1

C Greater than 1

D Negative **(2 marks)**

71 **H Co manufactures and sells a motor vehicle, the GHF300. Which of the following would cause an expansion in demand for this product in country M?**

A A reduction in the selling price of the GHF300

B The GHF300 becoming more fashionable with the public

C A reduction in direct taxes within country M

D An increase in the population of country M **(2 marks)**

72 **Which of the following is NOT a characteristic of a perfect market?**

A Large numbers of customers and suppliers

B All suppliers provide a wide range of products and services

C There is perfect information for customers and suppliers

D There are no entry or exit barriers to the market **(2 marks)**

73 **F operates in a market where it has only two major rivals – each of whom is roughly the same size as F. What type of market is F operating in?**

A Oligopoly

B Monopolistic competition **(1 mark)**

74 **Which of the following is a feature of monopolistic competition?**

A Few competitors in the market

B Undifferentiated products

C No major barriers to entry to or exit from the market

D Low advertising expenditure **(2 marks)**

75 Which of the following is NOT a factor that affects price elasticity of demand?

A The amount of customer income spent on item

B Duration of the price change

C The necessity of the item to consumers

D The initial number of units demanded **(2 marks)**

76 L makes a variety of different products, including windows. Which TWO of the following would cause a decrease in the level of supply of L's windows?

A An increase in the level of VAT charged by the government on windows

B A new automated assembly system for L's products that reduces L's window manufacturing overheads

C Staff negotiations, leading to window production staff adopting a shift-work approach which makes better use of L's production facilities

D Staff negotiations, leading to a slight rise in the hourly rate paid to window production workers **(2 marks)**

77 E Co manufactures a single product. Which of the following would indicate that the product will have a low price elasticity of demand?

A Customers spend a high proportion of their incomes on the product

B Customers don't see the product as being a necessity

C Customers tend to buy the product by habit

D Customers have a number of substitute products that they can choose from

(2 marks)

78 The government of country X is planning to introduce minimum wage legislation that would set minimum worker pay at significantly above the current average level of pay in the country. The labour market in country X is currently regarded as having reached its equilibrium point. Consider the following two statements regarding this legislation:

1 The legislation will likely increase the unemployment level within country X.

2 Manufacturers within country X will likely wish to make more labour-intensive products and reduce the amount of automation used within their businesses.

Which of these statements is/are correct?

A 1 only

B 2 only

C Both

D Neither **(2 marks)**

79 Freja is preparing a short-term budget for a cost incurred by her company. She is predicting that the company will experience significant increases in output during the period. How would Freja expect to see the average cost per unit change within the short-term?

A The cost per unit would be expected to fall for the entire period due to the increased output

B The cost per unit would be expected to initially fall, then start to rise again due to diseconomies of scale

C The cost per unit would be unlikely to change in the short-term

D The cost per unit would be expected to initially fall, then start to rise again due to the law of diminishing returns **(2 marks)**

80 Which of the following is the name given to unemployment which is the result of aggregate demand in the economy being too small to create employment opportunities for all those willing, and able, to work?

A Structural unemployment

B Cyclical unemployment

C Frictional unemployment

D Real wage unemployment **(2 marks)**

81 Rapid economic growth may lead to increased demand for imports.

Is this statement TRUE or FALSE?

A True

B False **(1 mark)**

82 Country Y has an increasingly high rate of unemployment. Which of the following statements is/are correct regarding the effect of this on consumers and businesses?

(i) Businesses may offer lower wages to staff

(ii) Government spending on social security will fall

(iii) Businesses will find it easier to locate new employees

(iv) Businesses may find that demand for their goods and services falls

A (i), (ii) and (iii) only

B (i), (iii) and (iv) only

C (i) and (iii) only

D All four are correct **(2 marks)**

83 Which of the following are typical macroeconomic policy objectives of governments?

	Yes	**No**
Economic growth		
Money supply management		

(2 marks)

84 Which of the following would best summarise the effect of expectations on a country's economy?

A Expectations effect has no influence on the economic development

B If a government is expecting the citizens' incomes to rise, it will try to adjust the taxation levels as to decrease the amount to be collected

C If a company expects its trade contract to be terminated, it will take actions to find another customer

D If people collectively expect the economy to develop in a certain way, they will act in a manner that will facilitate this change **(2 marks)**

85 What fiscal policy would be best used when trying to address a deflationary gap?

A Running a budget surplus

B Having a budget deficit

C Lowering interest rates

D Raising interest rates **(2 marks)**

86 Increases in unemployment, reduced demand, falling household incomes and low business confidence and investment are associated most strongly with which of the following?

A High interest rates

B Increase in the money supply

C A budget deficit

D Recession **(2 marks)**

87 If a government has a macroeconomic policy objective of expanding the overall level of economic activity, which of the following measure would be consistent with such an objective?

A Increasing public expenditure

B Increasing interest rates

C Increasing taxation **(1 mark)**

88 Which is the following is likely to be a result of a balance of payment surplus?

A Lower rate of economic growth

B Inflation

C Unemployment

D Budget deficit **(2 marks)**

89 Which of the following is a disadvantage of economic growth?

A Growth rates may exceed inflation rates

B The gap between rich and poor may narrow

C Growth may exceed population growth

D Growth may be in 'demerit' goods **(2 marks)**

90 Which of the following statements best describes demand-side policies?

A A belief that government should manipulate its spending so as to manage aggregate demand

B Ensuring that demand is contained so that inflation is controlled

C Managing down excessive growth by reducing government borrowing

D Keeping employment levels substantially below full levels **(2 marks)**

91 Country M is experiencing economic stagnation. A senior policy advisor has recently proposed that the nation should 'concentrate on limiting government intervention in markets and reducing fiscal deficits, rather than increasing public expenditure'.

Which economic theory is the policy advisor suggesting that country M should adopt?

A Classical

B Monetarist

C Keynesian

D Demand-side **(2 marks)**

92 Country C is experiencing a rising trade deficit. In addition, the costs of these imports are rising due to production problems in the countries that export to C. If all else stays constant, which two of the following would this be expected to cause?

(i) A fall in aggregate demand

(ii) Rising aggregate demand

(iii) Imported inflation

(iv) Monetary inflation

A (i) and (iii)

B (i) and (iv)

C (ii) and (iii)

D (ii) and (iv) **(2 marks)**

93 Which of the following would be classified as an expenditure-reducing strategy?

A Providing subsidies to exporters

B Lowering the currency exchange rate (devaluation)

C Running a budget surplus

D Import tariffs and quotas **(2 marks)**

94 Governments may need to intervene in the economy in order to move it nearer to its equilibrium point. Increased government expenditure and lower taxes can be used to stimulate demand and full employment is only possible with a boost from government policy and public investment.

Which approach to economics do these statements relate to?

A Keynesian

B Monetarist **(1 mark)**

EXTERNAL ANALYSIS – SOCIAL, ENVIRONMENTAL AND TECHNOLOGICAL FACTORS

95 Consider the following statements:

1 Monitoring population growth is usually only important for public or governmental organisations.

2 'Attitudes' represent an individual's personal preferences or patterns of choice.

Which of these statements is/are correct?

A 1 only

B 2 only

C Both

D Neither **(2 marks)**

96 Consider the following statements:

1 An aging population represents a risk to all businesses that manufacture or sell technologically advanced products.

2 Changes in social structure can have a significant impact on a country's buying patterns.

Which of these statements is/are correct?

A 1 only

B 2 only

C Both

D Neither **(2 marks)**

97 Outsourcing is often associated with which business processes?

A Allowing employees to work from home

B Sourcing data from outside the company

C Transferring call centres overseas

D Sending staff on foreign assignments **(2 marks)**

98 What change in people's attitudes has put additional pressure on businesses to become more socially responsible?

A Disposable income is growing as people have fewer children

B Urbanisation encourages companies to build more compact offices

C Fashion changes rapidly therefore frequently change of suppliers becomes a necessity

D People are more aware of the 'carbon footprint' left by a company's operations **(2 marks)**

99 Introduction of a new technology often means that a company can streamline its operations. This impacts organisational structure in which of the following ways?

A It encourages managers to spend more time controlling staff activities

B It allows the company to reorganise itself into a taller structure

C It allows delayering by widening a manager's span of control **(1 mark)**

100 Which of the following is NOT a way in which businesses can reduce the amount of damage they cause to the environment?

A Rebranding of products

B Recycling

C Redesigning products to use fewer materials

D Careful production planning **(2 marks)**

101 Organisations should use resources in such a way that they do not compromise the needs of future generations.

What is this a definition of?

A Environmentalism

B Sustainability

C Future-focus

D Redesign **(2 marks)**

102 Lannister is a bank based in country W. It is considering outsourcing its IT department to an overseas IT consultancy company. Its current IT systems are considered excellent, which is important as the banking industry in country W is highly competitive and innovative.

Which of the following statements regarding this proposal is correct?

A Outsourcing is likely to reduce the risk of data security breaches within Lannister

B Lannister is likely to enjoy increased in-house IT skills and knowledge

C Outsourcing Lannister's IT department could cause a loss of competitive advantage

D It is likely to be easy for Lannister to bring the IT function back in-house if problems arise with the IT consultancy company **(2 marks)**

103 Recycling waste material could be classed as being both environmentally friendly AND sustainable.

Is this statement TRUE or FALSE?

A True

B False **(1 mark)**

COMPETITIVE FACTORS

104 F Co sells motor vehicles in country V. It has recently discovered that the government is planning a major overhaul of the public transport system in country V, which will significantly increase its speed and comfort, while lowering the cost to make it attractive to individual drivers.

Under which heading of Porter's five forces model would this issue be included?

A Barriers to entry

B Power of suppliers

C Threat of substitutes

D Power of buyers **(2 marks)**

105 X Co offers accountancy training courses. The market is growing quickly and X's courses are significantly different to those offered by its rivals. Any new company wishing to teach accountancy courses must obtain accreditation by the various accountancy organisations – a process which can take several years.

Based on the above information, which of the following statements can be made about X's competitive environment?

A Competitive rivalry is likely to be low

B Supplier power is likely to be low

C Barriers to entry are likely to be low

D The threat of new entrants is likely to be low **(2 marks)**

106 Which of the following factors would most significantly increase the threat of new entrants into an industry?

A Strong government regulation requiring extensive permits

B High capital requirements for starting operations

C Low customer switching costs between competing products

D Existing firms hold large amounts of confidential product knowledge **(2 marks)**

107 When considering Porter's value chain analysis, which of the following describes outbound logistics?

A receiving, handling and distributing inputs to the production system

B using rational approach to solving problems

C informing customers about the products a company has to offer

D distributing the products to the customer **(2 marks)**

108 AAH Co buys cable from a number of manufacturers, cuts it into shorter lengths and sells it to various retailers. One of its departments is solely responsible for the cutting of the cable.

Which of Porter's value chain activities is the department responsible for?

A Procurement

B Operations

C Inbound logistics

D Infrastructure **(2 marks)**

109 A company who sells its product at a price below that of similar rival products is likely to have adopted a differentiation strategy.

Is this statement TRUE or FALSE?

A True

B False **(1 mark)**

110 H provides a range of products and services that are tailored specifically to pregnant women.

What type of strategy is H adopting?

A Focus

B Differentiation **(1 mark)**

111 **Porter's value chain determines whether and how a firm's activities contribute to which of the following?**

A its long term survival

B its competitive advantage

C its profitability

D its productive capacity **(2 marks)**

112 BCD Co is a large trading company. Steve is the administration manager and is also responsible for legal and compliance functions. Sheila is responsible for customer service and has responsibility for ensuring that customers who have purchased goods from BCD Co are fully satisfied. Sunny deals with suppliers and negotiates on the price and quality of inventory. He is also responsible for identifying the most appropriate suppliers of plant and machinery for the factory. Sam is the information technology manager and is responsible for all information systems within the company.

According to Porter's value chain, which of the managers is involved in a primary activity as opposed to a support activity?

A Steve

B Sheila

C Sunny

D Sam **(2 marks)**

113 AZ Co is performing a SWOT analysis and notes that it has a large cash balance. Which of the SWOT headings would this be most likely to fall under?

A Strengths

B Weaknesses

C Opportunities

D Threats **(2 marks)**

114 A value network looks at the linkages between the supply chains of different organisations – such as suppliers and their customers.

Is this statement TRUE or FALSE?

A True

B False **(1 mark)**

PROFESSIONAL ETHICS IN ACCOUNTING AND BUSINESS

115 Amelia is an accountant for LGH Co, a large multinational organisation. She has recently been accused of theft from the company. She has argued that the theft was justified as she needed the money to care for her mother, who is seriously ill.

What approach to ethics has Amelia adopted?

A Pluralist

B Utilitarian

C Absolutist

D Relativist **(2 marks)**

116 A profession must have an ethical code to which it requires compliance.

Is this statement TRUE or FALSE?

A True

B False **(1 mark)**

117 ACCA members are required to comply with five Fundamental Principles. Which of the following contains three of these principles?

A Integrity, Objectivity, Honesty

B Professional competence and due care, Professional behaviour, Confidentiality

C Social responsibility, Independence, Scepticism

D Courtesy, Reliability, Responsibility **(2 marks)**

118 Are the following statements true or false?

Statement	**True**	**False**
All ACCA members must comply with the Fundamental Principles, whether or not they are in practice.		
Professionals owe an obligation to society as well as a duty to their client.		

(2 marks)

119 Objectivity means that accountants must not be associated with any false or misleading statements.

Is this statement TRUE or FALSE?

A True

B False **(1 mark)**

120 Jack is an employee in BBB Co. He has been offered a bribe by an existing supplier to continue buying a key component used in BBB's manufacturing process from them, in spite of a new rival company offering the same component at a significantly lower price.

Which of the following statements regarding Jack's decision is correct?

A If Jack is an egoist, he will most likely accept the bribe

B If Jack is a relativist, he would refuse the bribe as bribery is always wrong

C If Jack is a utilitarian, he would reject the bribe as it does not benefit all stakeholders

D If Jack is an absolutist, his decision would depend on the circumstances **(2 marks)**

121 Which of the following would be seen as a difference between a profession and an occupation?

A An occupation is governed by a professional body

B Members of a profession must comply with relevant legislation

C To be classified as an occupation, members must follow an ethical code

D Members of a profession must go through a process of certification **(2 marks)**

122 Mia has uncovered fraudulent activity within the company she works for. Who should she alert about this matter first?

A Her professional accountancy body

B The company's major shareholders

C Her company's Compliance Officer

D The relevant authorities **(2 marks)**

123 Noor is an ACCA member. Last year one of her clients, Aron, asked her to value a business that he wished to purchase. She did so and informed Aron that the business was competitively priced. Aron subsequently bought the business for its full asking price of several million pounds. This year, Aron has become concerned that the business has been underperforming and has asked Noor to reassess its performance and long-term prospects.

Which type of ethical threat is Noor facing?

A Self-interest

B Self-review

C Advocacy

D Intimidation **(2 marks)**

124 Which of the following are NOT safeguards that the ACCA and other professional bodies put in place to attempt to eliminate ethical threats?

A Ethics training

B Internal complaints procedures

C Creation of corporate governance regulations

D Professional monitoring and disciplinary procedures **(2 marks)**

125 Lorenzo is facing an ethical dilemma. When deciding what his course of action should be, he is concerned with making sure that the outcome of his decision will benefit the greatest number of people.

Which approach to ethical decision-making is Lorenzo following?

A Egoist

B Utilitarian

C Pluralist

D Individualist **(2 marks)**

126 Which of the following is a value that organisations try to encourage within their corporate culture in order to encourage staff to act ethically?

A Empowerment

B Integrity

C Satisfaction

D Objectivity **(2 marks)**

127 In order to encourage ethical behaviour, BHG Co has told all of its employees that they must treat all employees and stakeholders well, regardless of their gender, age, ethnicity or sexuality. Which key value is BHG asking its staff to consider?

A Empowerment

B Trust

C Respect

D Honesty **(2 marks)**

128 Deontological ethics suggest that the consequences of an action should be ignored.

Is this statement TRUE or FALSE?

A True

B False **(1 mark)**

GOVERNANCE AND SOCIAL RESPONSIBILITY IN BUSINESS

129 Where there are a large number of external shareholders who play no role in the day-to-day running of a company, there is a situation that is described as:

A detached corporate ownership

B uninvolved external ownership

C dividend based shareholding

D separation of ownership and management **(2 marks)**

130 The 'agency problem' refers to which of the following situations?

A Shareholders acting in their own short-term interests rather than the long-term interests of the company

B A vocal minority of shareholders expecting the directors to act as their agents and pay substantial dividends

C Companies reliant upon substantial government contracts such that they are effectively agents of the government

D The directors acting in their own interests rather than the shareholders' interests **(2 marks)**

131 To encourage Executive Directors to operate in the best interests of the shareholders, they could:

A be given a high basic salary

B receive share options based on both individual and company's performance

C be entitled to large payment upon resignation or termination

D be asked to attend AGMs **(2 marks)**

132 Corporate social responsibility refers to the idea that a company should:

A play an active part in the social life of the local neighbourhood

B be sensitive to the needs of all stakeholders

C be alert to the social needs of all employees

D act responsibly in relation to shareholders' overall needs – not just their financial needs **(2 marks)**

133 Which of the following would best explain the concept of sustainable development?

A Starting business in developed countries where the economic climate is conducive to trade

B Development which meets the needs of the present without compromising the ability of future generations to meet their own needs

C Sustaining the production at the level of maximum capacity

D Developing the business by signing long-term contracts with suppliers **(2 marks)**

134 Modern view on Corporate Social Responsibility is:

A it is a way to further a company's business and attract additional shareholders

B it is necessary to reduce product liability claims

C a company must give part of its profits to charity

D social responsibility is incompatible with the objective of maximising shareholder's wealth **(2 marks)**

135 The agency problem refers to the fact that shareholders cannot legally be the directors of an organisation.

Is this statement TRUE or FALSE?

A True

B False **(1 mark)**

136 Which of the following would render a non-executive director of a company less suitable for this post?

A The person worked for the company six years ago

B The person has served as a non-executive for the last six years

C The person has no previous contact with the executive directors

D The person owns a number of the company's shares **(2 marks)**

137 An audit committee should:

A consist of independent non-executive directors only

B include at least one senior member of the internal audit team

C include one member from the external audit firm

D carry out a detailed review of critical elements of the statement of financial position **(2 marks)**

138 The most obvious means of achieving public oversight of corporate governance is via:

A the company establishing a comprehensive web site

B publication of the Annual Report and Accounts

C press announcements of all significant developments

D shareholder access to the Annual General Meeting **(2 marks)**

139 Within the UK, what is the usual purpose of codes of practice on corporate governance?

A To establish legally binding requirements to which all companies must adhere

B To set down detailed rules to regulate the ways in which companies must operate

C To provide guidance on the standards of best practice that companies should adopt

D To provide a comprehensive framework for management and administration

(2 marks)

140 Which of the following types of committee is often temporary in nature and is formed to complete a particular task?

A ad-hoc committee

B standing committee

C executive committee

D sub-committee **(2 marks)**

141 Which of the following would normally be included in the role of a Committee Chair?

A Making administrative arrangements

B Dealing with correspondence

C Issuing the agenda

D Ensuring correct procedures are followed **(2 marks)**

142 The duties of the committee secretary include which of the following?

A Making notes/Issuing documents/Fixing date, time, location/Deciding who is to speak

B Fixing date, time and location/Making notes/Issuing documents/Preparing minutes

C Making notes/Issuing documents/Preparing minutes/Maintaining order

D Issuing documents/Fixing date, time, location/Ascertaining the consensus view/ Preparing minutes **(2 marks)**

143 As a requirement of the UK Corporate Governance Code, the remuneration committee of a large company determines the:

1 rates of pay

2 grades

for all of the company's staff.

Which of the two options given are correct?

A 1 only

B 2 only

C Both

D Neither **(2 marks)**

144 Committees typically make decisions more quickly than individuals as they create a larger pool of skills and knowledge.

Is this statement TRUE or FALSE?

A True

B False **(1 mark)**

145 Committees may fail to recommend decisive action where needed, due to the need for compromise between members.

Is this statement TRUE or FALSE?

A True

B False **(1 mark)**

LAW AND REGULATION GOVERNING ACCOUNTING

146 When submitting annual financial statements to be available for inspection by third parties, a company should send them to:

A Stock exchange

B Tax authorities

C Shareholders

D Companies house **(2 marks)**

147 The preparation and filing of accounts by companies each year is normally required by which of the following?

A Codes of corporate governance

B National legislation

C International Accounting Standards

D IFAC **(2 marks)**

148 L Co has recently prepared its draft financial statements for the last financial year. It has been informed by its auditors that these financial statements are not 'true and fair'. Which of the following would NOT have caused this?

A L failed to follow generally-accepted practice in the preparation of its financial statements

B L's financial statements did not set out relevant information in sufficient detail

C L failed to follow all appropriate accounting standards in the preparation of its financial statements

D L's financial statements contained minor errors **(2 marks)**

149 FVF Co is a listed company in country N. Regulators have recently discovered that the company has failed to maintain proper accounting records, meaning that the financial statements in recent years have not been true and fair.

Which of the following could be among the consequences of this failure?

	Yes	**No**
Suspension of FVF's shares by the stock exchange.		
Tax authority investigation into FVF.		

(2 marks)

150 The key aim of the International Accounting Standards Board (IASB) is to:

A Improve the standards of financial reporting worldwide

B Develop worldwide auditing standards

C Develop a single set of high-quality global accounting standards

D Represent UK interests effectively in financial reporting matters **(2 marks)**

151 Which of the following is the primary responsibility of the IFRS Interpretations Committee (IFRS IC)?

A Advising the IASB on agenda decisions and priorities in their work

B Review of newly identified accounting issues on a timely basis and provision of guidance on these issues

C The development and publication of IFRSs and other publications

D Informing the IASB of the views of the Council with regards to major standard-setting projects **(2 marks)**

152 Which of the following statements regarding UK accounting regulation is/are correct?

1 The Supervision Committee is responsible for the creation of UK Financial Reporting Standards (FRSs).

2 In the UK, Statements of Standard Accounting Practice (SSAPs) have been largely replaced by Financial Reporting Standards (FRSs).

A 1 only

B 2 only

C Both

D Neither **(2 marks)**

ACCOUNTING AND FINANCE FUNCTIONS WITHIN BUSINESS

153 In a very large company managing the total level of working capital would probably be the responsibility of the:

A Finance director

B Chief accountant

C Treasurer

D Management accountant **(2 marks)**

154 Financial accountants usually produce information for the organisation's external stakeholders.

Is this statement TRUE or FALSE?

A True

B False **(1 mark)**

155 There is no legal requirement for companies to have a management accounting function.

Is this statement TRUE or FALSE?

A True

B False **(1 mark)**

156 A is a small owner-managed company employing 20 staff and having a revenue of 300,000 Euro a year. It decided not to appoint external auditors to review its financial statements. Such a decision:

A is in line with the requirements of current legislations

B will be criticised by governmental authorities

C will allow the company to strengthen its financial controls **(1 mark)**

157 Which of the following tasks would the treasury department be responsible for?

A Recording financial transactions

B Managing foreign currency exposure

C Reporting to shareholders

D Putting together standard cost cards **(2 marks)**

158 Gabriella is considering creating a financial accounting department within her business, but is unsure of what such a department would actually do. Which of the following would usually be prepared by a financial accounting department?

A Cost schedules

B Statement of cash flows

C Variance analysis

D Tax calculations **(2 marks)**

159 Angelo decided to record the purchases made on the 2nd of April 200X in the tax year ending 31st of March 200X. The authorities will likely classify this as tax ____________.

Which of the following words correctly fill this gap?

evasion/minimisation/avoidance*

*delete as appropriate **(1 mark)**

160 Tax mitigation involves which of the following?

A Taking all legal steps to reduce one's tax liability

B Agreeing to pay a financial penalty to avoid prosecution

C Moving businesses and funds offshore to reduce liability to UK tax

D Reducing tax liabilities without frustrating the law makers' intentions **(2 marks)**

161 An important advantage of using loans to finance investment is:

A loan interest payments can usually be suspended if profits are low

B the timing of loan payments is often at the company's discretion

C loan interest is tax deductible

D banks will often not require security for loan advances **(2 marks)**

162 VDF Co is planning to raise finance to fund the launch of a new product. It is planning to do this via an issue of new shares to the public. Which of the following is an issue that VDF may face if it proceeds with its plans to raise equity finance?

A It will be forced to pay higher dividends in the future – even if the new product launch is a failure

B The share issue may dilute the control that the existing shareholders have over the company

C VDF will require good quality assets to offer as security for the new issue

D The issue of shares is likely to reduce VDF's corporation tax liability **(2 marks)**

163 Working capital is calculated as:

A the excess of current assets over current liabilities

B the excess of bank borrowings over current assets

C the excess of long-term liabilities over short-term liabilities

D the excess of fixed assets over current assets **(2 marks)**

164 Which of the following statements regarding management accounting reports is correct?

A Budgets show the revenues and expenditure for the last accounting period

B Cost schedules are often also referred to as standard cost cards

C Variance reports compare the original budgets to revised budgets

D Management accountants will usually be responsible for creation of the statement of financial position **(2 marks)**

165 Which of the following statements regarding integrated reports is correct?

A They involve the merging of the other financial statements to produce an overall view of company performance

B They are designed to show the organisation's profitability more clearly

C They include information on anything that is felt to be of interest to the users of the financial statements

D They include only relevant financial information for the users of the financial statements **(2 marks)**

166 Which of the following is NOT one of the purposes of budgets?

A responsibility for expenditure

B motivation of employees

C co-ordination of staff

D costing of units **(2 marks)**

167 Which of the following is NOT one of the "capitals" used in integrated reporting?

A Intellectual capital

B Environmental capital

C Natural capital

D Human capital **(2 marks)**

168 Daniel is trying to find certain key figures from the financial statements of HGF Co. He is unsure about whether to look at the Statement of Financial Position (SOFP) or the Statement or profit or loss (SOPL) for each one.

Which section of the financial statements will the following information be found?

	SOPL	**SOFP**
The net assets of HGF		
HGF's gross profit for the year		

(2 marks)

FINANCIAL SYSTEMS AND PROCEDURES

169 Victoria runs a business which sells computer equipment. She is concerned that when her business pays its suppliers, the wrong amount may be paid. Which of the following control measures could help Victoria to deal with this problem?

A Regular supplier statement reconciliations

B Match the GRN to the original purchase order sent to the supplier

C Matching of the purchase order to the requisition order

D Prompt recording of invoices received **(2 marks)**

170 JBB Co manufactures and sells furniture, which it sells online and delivers to customers. JBB has recently faced a number of complaints from customers who have been sent the wrong style or colour of furniture.

Which of the following controls would help JBB to avoid this problem?

(i) Agree goods despatched note (GDN) to original order

(ii) Match invoice to GDN

(iii) Match orders sent to invoices raised

(iv) Send confirmation of receivables to customers

A (i) only

B (i) and (ii) only

C (i) and (iii) only

D (ii) and (iv) only **(2 marks)**

171 Noah is considering introducing a number of control systems into his business. However, he is uncertain about what this would accomplish. Which of the following is NOT a purpose of organisational control systems?

A Safeguarding of company assets

B Prevention of errors

C Increased profitability

D Increased efficiency **(2 marks)**

172 Which of the following would ensure that the sales cycle results in prompt payment?

A Orders are processed by qualified personnel only

B Checking the goods are in inventory before dispatching them

C Each item has its own code

D Checking the creditworthiness of the customer **(2 marks)**

173 The most secure and easy way to verify payments to staff is by:

A authorising payments before they are made

B using BACS transfers

C paying people in cash

D asking staff to visit the accounts office to receive their wages **(2 marks)**

174 Grey Ltd has recently discovered that it has been paying invoices in respect of goods which had been returned as faulty before acceptance. It is company policy to record goods only if they have been accepted. Which of the following controls would have prevented this from occurring?

A Matching purchase invoices with goods received records

B Matching purchase invoices with orders

C Comparison of supplier statements with payables ledger accounts

D Date stamping purchase invoices on receipt. **(2 marks)**

175 Consider the following two statements:

1 When petty cash is replenished, it is usual for the amount of cash withdrawn to equal the value of the receipts and vouchers produced since the previous replenishment.

2 It would be best practice for a company that predominantly receives cheques and postal orders in payment for goods dispatched to appoint a single, designated and trusted individual to open the mail.

Which of these statements is/are correct?

A 1 only

B 2 only

C Both

D Neither **(2 marks)**

176 Reducing the incidence of fraud is primarily an issue of:

A security arrangements

B system procedures

C recruitment procedures

D organisational control **(2 marks)**

THE RELATIONSHIP BETWEEN ACCOUNTING AND OTHER BUSINESS FUNCTIONS

177 E Co has a large marketing department. In which of the following ways would this department co-ordinate with E's accounting department?

A Decisions on the quantity of raw materials required

B Establishing credit terms for customers

C Calculating pay rises for staff

D Decisions on the selling price of the product **(2 marks)**

178 Which of the following is NOT a way in which an organisation's production department would co-ordinate with its accounting department?

A Calculating charge out rates for services provided by the organisation

B Calculating the budgets for the number of units to be produced

C Estimation of the costs of the raw materials required for production

D Decisions on the quality of raw materials that the organisation can afford to use **(2 marks)**

179 'Services have certain qualities which distinguish them from products. Due to their _____________, physical elements such as tickets, confirmations and certificates are important part of the service provision.'

Which word fits the gap in the above definition?

inseparability/intangibility/perishability/variability*

*delete as appropriate **(2 marks)**

180 HGF is a company that operates taxis within several cities in country U and has received a number of complaints regarding the behaviour of its drivers towards passengers. One of HGF's marketing executives has pointed out that even if the customer's journey is fast, cheap and reliable, customers will still see the service offered by HGF as poor if the driver behaves poorly.

What aspect of the nature of service provision is HGF's marketing executive referring to?

A Intangibility

B Perishability

C Variability

D Inseparability **(2 marks)**

AUDIT AND FINANCIAL CONTROL

181 The key purpose of internal auditing is to:

A detect errors and fraud

B evaluate the organisation's risk management processes and systems of control

C give confidence as to the truth and fairness of the financial statements

D express an internal opinion on the truth and fairness of the financial statements **(2 marks)**

182 Internal check is defined as:

1 ensuring that no single task is executed from start to finish by only one person.

2 providing reasonable assurance about the achievement of the organisation's objectives.

Which of these options is/are correct?

A 1 only

B 2 only

C Both

D Neither **(2 marks)**

183 Internal auditors have an unavoidable .... problem, as they report to those people whose activities they are reporting on.

Which word correctly completes this sentence?

A Integrity

B Independence

C Loyalty **(2 marks)**

184 **It is considered to be best practice for the internal auditors of a large company to report directly to:**

A the board of directors

B the external auditors

C the shareholders

D the audit committee **(2 marks)**

185 Emma is preparing a seminar for the Board of Directors of the company she works for regarding internal and external audit and the differences between the two.

Which TWO of the following points are correct with regards to internal and external audit?

A The scope of the internal auditors' work is determined by the management of the company, while external auditors determine the scope of their own work

B Internal auditors test the organisation's underlying transactions, while external auditors test the operations of the organisation's systems

C Internal audit and external audit are usually both legal requirements

D Internal auditors can be employees of the company they audit, while external auditors must not be **(2 marks)**

186 Consider the following two statements:

1 There is greater flexibility in how internal audit work is done relative to external audit work, since external audit work is controlled by the law and audit standards.

2 To practice as an internal auditor, the person must be a qualified accountant.

Which of these options is/are correct?

A 1 only

B 2 only

C Both

D Neither **(2 marks)**

187 The fact that managers are not aware of problems a company is facing, such as not knowing that a major incident of fraud has recently taken place, would weaken which of the following components of internal controls?

A Control environment

B The entity's risk assessment process

C Control activities

D The entity's process to monitor the system of internal control **(2 marks)**

188 A retail company operates a transaction processing system (TPS). Which component of internal control would this be a part of?

A The entity's risk assessment process

B The entity's process to monitor the system of internal control

C Control environment

D Information systems and communication **(2 marks)**

189 Consider the following statements regarding control activities:

1 The primary purpose of the segregation of duties between individuals within the organisation is to locate and identify frauds that employees have perpetrated.

2 'General' computer controls include physical controls to prevent unauthorised access to computer equipment, such as door locks and card entry systems.

Which of these options is/are correct?

A 1 only

B 2 only

C Both

D Neither **(2 marks)**

190 Jana is the payables clerk in a large manufacturing organisation. One of her duties is to record purchase orders but she is not authorised to make payments to suppliers. This is an example of the important general principle known as:

A controlled record access

B segregation of duties

C dual control

D initiation control **(2 marks)**

191 Users of a company's internal network are restricted to read-only access to key folders. What type of control is this an example of?

A Preventive

B Detective

C Corrective

D Physical **(2 marks)**

192 Lucas is entering customer details onto a computer system. The system requires him to log in and checks that he is allowed to enter customer details. The system also checks that he has entered all the required information about the customer.

These computer system controls will NOT ensure which of the following?

A Completeness

B Authorisation

C Validity

D Identification **(2 marks)**

193 Which TWO of the following are examples of general controls within IT systems?

A Physical – such as protection against power surges

B Logical – such as password systems

C Forensic – such as audit trails for all transactions **(1 mark)**

194 Which of the following would be most likely to be classed as a preventive control?

A Having a supervisor present on the shop floor at all times

B Conducting regular receivables statement reconciliations

C Year-end inventory checks

D Establishing procedures for irrecoverable debt collection **(2 marks)**

195 Consider the following two statements:

1 Responsibility for the internal controls is shared between management and the internal auditors.

2 The internal auditor's role often includes helping to set corporate objectives and the design and monitoring of performance measures.

Which of these options is/are correct?

A 1 only

B 2 only

C Both

D Neither **(2 marks)**

196 Which of the following statements are correct with regards to external audit?

(i) Due to their in-depth examination of the business, external auditors are often able to provide advice to management on possible improvements to the business.

(ii) External auditors often have an independence problem as they report to management and yet are also expected to give an objective opinion on them.

(iii) External audits can help to resolve management disputes, such as disagreements over company valuations or profit-sharing agreements.

(iv) External auditors have little or no interest in the internal controls of the organisation as these are the responsibility of the internal auditors.

A (i) and (iii)

B (i), (ii) and (iv)

C (i), (iii) and (iv)

D (ii) and (iv) **(2 marks)**

197 Every evening the last person leaving the office premises needs to switch on the security alarm. This control belongs to which of the following categories?

A Authorisation

B Verification

C Reconciliation

D Physical or logical **(2 marks)**

198 Controls that are fully automated and are designed to ensure that the data input into a system is complete and accurate are known as:

A General controls

B Information processing controls **(1 mark)**

199 External auditors have no interest in the internal controls of the organisation they are auditing.

Is this statement TRUE or FALSE?

A True

B False **(1 mark)**

FRAUD, FRAUDULENT BEHAVIOUR AND THEIR PREVENTION IN BUSINESS

200 Which of the following are considered to be the three prerequisites for fraud to occur?

	Yes	No
Motivation		
Opportunity		

(2 marks)

201 Which of the following is a skimming fraud?

A A large amount is 'skimmed' off the top of a large sales invoice as a kickback to the purchaser

B Small amounts are diverted from a large number of transactions

C Invitation to pay a sum of money now in order to secure a large return in the future

D Submission of invoices which contain inflated amounts **(2 marks)**

202 'Teeming and lading' is used to describe which of the following:

A Where money flows are so substantial that diversion of large sums can go unnoticed

B A fraud where purchase ledger payments are misdirected to overseas accounts

C A personal expenses fraud involving fictitious expense vouchers

D A fraud where receipts from customers are misappropriated **(2 marks)**

203 'Window dressing' involves which of the following:

A Producing an overly detailed set of annual accounts in years when underlying results are poor

B Entering into transactions just before the year-end that will improve the appearance of the accounts but will be reversed out soon after

C Setting up bogus employees on the payroll system and paying their 'salary' into a specially created bank account

D Misappropriation of business assets by managers **(2 marks)**

204 Off balance sheet accounting refers to which of the following:

A A focus on income and expenditure rather to the detriment of asset and liability management

B Removal of business assets by employees for their own personal use

C Diversion of assets from the balance sheet to a personal bank account

D Deliberate exclusion of certain assets and liabilities from the published balance sheet **(2 marks)**

205 Consider the following two statements:

1 A comprehensive system of control will eliminate all fraud and error.

2 Employees working in departments other than Accounts have no responsibility for reporting fraud.

Which of these options is/are correct?

A 1 only

B 2 only

C Both

D Neither **(2 marks)**

206 If an external auditor in the process of considering the company's financial statements came across an incident of fraud that took place in the year, they must:

A issue a modified opinion on the accounts regardless of the size of the fraud

B report to the shareholders by way of a note to the accounts, regardless of the size of the fraud

C issue a modified opinion on the accounts only if the fraud is material and not properly recorded in the accounts

D report to the shareholders by way of a note to the accounts, but only if the fraud is material **(2 marks)**

207 Which of the following behaviours is often associated with an employee possibly committing fraud?

A Managers and staff having monthly meetings to discuss underperformance

B Employee frequently taking time off work for personal reasons

C A member of the Finance team frequently buying new expensive cars despite only earning a moderate salary

D Member of HR team being keen to take part in discussion on staff remuneration **(2 marks)**

208 Which of the following is NOT a control or procedure required by standard money laundering legislation?

A Identification of large or unusual transactions

B Taking steps to ensure customers can be identified

C Reporting of all large or unusual transactions to the relevant authorities

D Creation of the role of Nominated Officer **(2 marks)**

209 Money laundering legislation only covers illegally obtained cash and other liquid assets, such as short-term investments and bonds.

Is this statement TRUE or FALSE?

A True

B False **(1 mark)**

210 Under typical money laundering legislation, the main offences recognised are: placement, layering and integration.

Is this statement TRUE or FALSE?

A True

B False **(1 mark)**

211 Lack of control over which of the following activities can lead to the fraudulent activity of teeming and lading?

A Non-current asset register

B Budgetary system

C Inventory management

D Sales ledger and receipts **(2 marks)**

212 Leo has been offering investors in his company a 15% per annum return on their investment. In order to fund this return, Leo has been using money raised from newer investors to pay the 15% returns demanded by early investors.

What type of fraud is Leo committing?

A Manipulation of revenue recognition

B Advance fee fraud

C False billing fraud

D Ponzi scheme **(2 marks)**

213 BNG Co has recently discovered that it has been the victim of a false-billing fraud. Which of the following controls could BNG put in place to prevent this from occurring in the future?

A Segregation of duties within the accounts department

B Online payments made directly into suppliers' bank account

C Authorisation of payments by management

D Maintenance of a regular trial balance **(2 marks)**

LEADERSHIP, MANAGEMENT AND SUPERVISION

214 Harry is a manager at GHF Co. He does not get on well with the employees who report to him and has little real power to punish or reward the staff for their behaviour. Which of the following management styles does Fiedler suggest would work best for Harry?

A Psychologically close

B Psychologically open

C Psychologically committed

D Psychologically distant **(2 marks)**

215 Responsibility can be delegated by management, as long as they also delegate sufficient authority.

Is this statement TRUE or FALSE?

A True

B False **(1 mark)**

216 Management is the effective use and co-ordination of business resources in order to achieve key objectives with maximum efficiency.

Is this statement TRUE or FALSE?

A True

B False **(1 mark)**

217 The main role of a supervisor is best described as:

A a negotiator of industrial relations within a department

B someone to resolve problems first hand where the work is done

C someone to ensure that specified tasks are performed correctly and efficiently

D the interface between junior and senior managers **(2 marks)**

218 KJA Co manufactures motorbikes. Which of the following statements is consistent with Taylor's theory of management?

A KJA should create employee suggestion schemes to generate ideas for how to improve its operations

B KJA should focus on improving group relations and team spirit within its workforce

C KJA does not need to set detailed standards for hiring workers as it should provide detailed training for all new employees

D KJA's managers should make all key decisions and provide detailed instructions to workers **(2 marks)**

219 Which of the following is delegated from a superior, Adam, to his subordinate, Helen?

A Authority

B Power

C Responsibility **(1 mark)**

220 Which of the following are the THREE main categories used by Mintzberg to group the ten skills that managers need?

(i) Interpersonal

(ii) Decisional

(iii) Informational

(iv) Individual

A (i), (ii) and (iv)

B (i), (iii) and (iv)

C (i), (ii) and (iii)

D (ii), (iii) and (iv) **(2 marks)**

221 Fayol defined authority as the:

1 Right to give orders

2 Power to exact obedience

3 Ability to force workers to follow orders

4 Ability to delegate responsibility

Which of these statements are correct?

A 1 and 2

B 2 and 3

C 3 and 4

D 2 and 4) **(2 marks)**

222 The senior management of GFD Co feel that their main role within the business is to ensure that all employees are working towards achieving the company's goals. Which of Fayol's five functions of management are the management focussing on?

A Planning

B Organising

C Commanding

D Co-ordinating **(2 marks)**

223 Ella is a manager in the purchasing department of Gamma Ltd. She is planning to introduce a new computer system into the department. Ella plans to offer staff bonuses to encourage her staff to use the new system, as well as relying on her own personal charisma.

Which TWO of the following sources of power is Ella planning to use?

A Reward

B Legitimate

C Referent

D Coercive **(2 marks)**

224 In the context of Blake and Mouton's grid a manager in the top left hand corner of the grid (1, 9) would fall into which of the following categories?

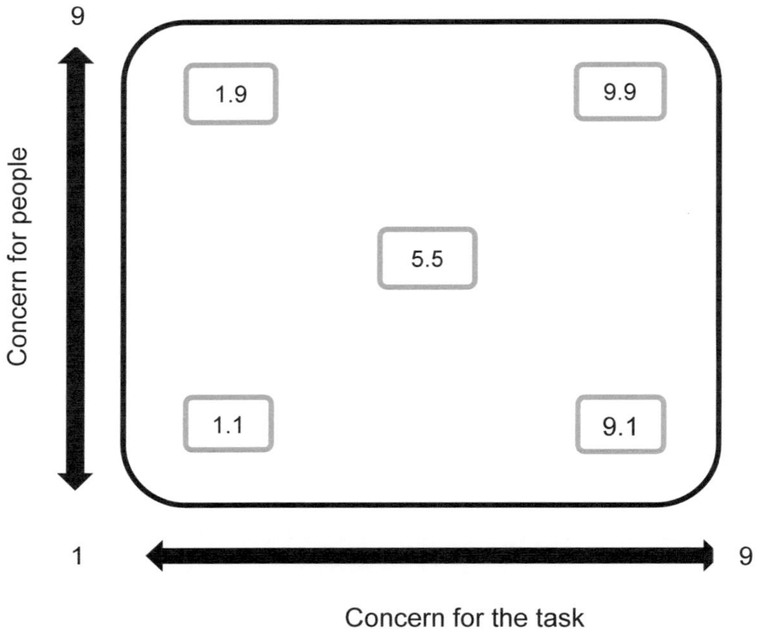

A Management impoverished

B 'Country Club'

C Task management

D Team management **(2 marks)**

225 Christina is planning to introduce a new IT system within her department, but is unsure about which system to purchase. She has asked the junior staff within the department to give her their opinions. However, Christina retains the final say in which system is to be purchased.

According to the Ashridge Management College, what management style is Christina adopting?

A Joins

B Tells

C Consults

D Sells **(2 marks)**

226 Consider the following two statements:

1 According to Bennis, transactional leaders offer rewards to their followers in exchange for their compliance.

2 Trait theories of management suggest that certain leadership approaches can be learnt and used by managers.

Which of these options is/are correct?

A 1 only

B 2 only

C Both

D Neither **(2 marks)**

INDIVIDUAL, GROUP AND TEAM BEHAVIOUR

227 When checking sales records of the company, a junior member of staff has uncovered a suspicious irregularity in the way transactions are processed. This would need more time to be investigated fully, however the audit manager is stressing the need to meet the tight deadline for completion. Using the role theory, this could be referred to as:

A role ambiguity

B role sign

C role behaviour

D role conflict **(2 marks)**

228 Waiters in a restaurant have been told that they have to wear black suits and bow ties so that can be easily identified by customers. What aspect of role theory does this relate to?

A Role behaviour

B Role signs

C Role set

D Role definition **(2 marks)**

229

Statement	**True**	**False**
Assertive behaviour often leads to conflict within an organisation.		
Individuals usually join informal groups on a voluntary basis.		

(2 marks)

230 Which of the following statements is correct with regards to the differences between individuals and teams?

A Teams tend to enjoy synergies which cannot be achieved by individual workers

B Teams tend to make decisions more rapidly than individuals

C Individuals are less likely to make definite decisions and rely on compromises

D There are fewer controls in place when groups make decisions **(2 marks)**

231 A manager in a business has discovered that several of their employees meet after work to socialise. Which of the following features would indicate that these employees are a group, rather than a team?

A They are committed to achieving a given objective

B They are made up of diverse individuals

C They have a sense of group identity

D Their focus is mainly social in nature, with no defined goal **(2 marks)**

232 Which of the following includes three of the roles Belbin suggested a group needs in order to be effective?

A Leader, Shaper, Plant

B Negotiator; Finisher; Initiator

C Co-ordinator; Progress chaser; Diplomat

D Finisher; Block remover; Negotiator **(2 marks)**

233 Match the following team roles with the appropriate personality.

(i) Sarah is a very quiet person, she often reserves her opinion until being directly asked for it however she always offers unusual and creative suggestions when the team is faced with difficult problem.

(ii) Jim is respected by all team members for his analytical skills, though he rarely gets invited to out-of-office private parties as many find him tactless.

(iii) Esther is the company's HR manager, she ensures that any potential conflicts are promptly identified and resolved and the team members work harmoniously.

A 1 – Shaper, 2 – Leader, 3 – Company worker

B 1 – Plant, 2 – Finisher, 3 – Team worker

C 1 – Plant, 2 – Monitor-Evaluator, 3 – Team worker

D 1 – Resource-Investigator, 2 – Shaper, 3 – Company worker **(2 marks)**

234 Which is the stage of team development during which the effectiveness of work will be at the lowest point according to Tuckman?

A Performing

B Storming

C Forming

D Norming **(2 marks)**

235 The fifth stage which has been added to Tuckman's four stages of team development is:

A Warming

B Reforming

C Dorming

D Leading **(2 marks)**

236 Jana manages a team of workers within her department. She has recently sat in on a team meeting during which the team had started discussing which roles each team member would take on.

Which of Tuckman's stages of group development does Jana's team appear to have reached?

A Storming

B Norming

C Performing

D Forming **(2 marks)**

237 An investment bank has created a team of employees to look at potential new investments. One of the bank's senior managers has told the team that they will be assessed on their performance as a group. Which of the following is NOT a possible risk to the bank of this approach?

A Lack of individual responsibility leads the group to make risky decisions

B Some members may put in little effort due to the lack of individual appraisal

C Group members may agree to poor decisions merely to 'fit in' with the group

D The group may have diverse backgrounds from within the bank **(2 marks)**

238 Louis is a member of a project team. His colleagues in the team rely on him to read and check complex project documentation. Louis has a keen eye for detail and often identifies minor details in documents that others miss but may be of significance. Despite this diligent approach, Louis always meets his deadlines. However, Some of Louis's colleagues feel frustrated when he refuses to involve others. He can hold up progress as he will not agree to the team signing off project documents until all of his concerns are fully discussed.

According to Belbin's team roles theory, Louis is an example of which of the following?

A Implementer

B Completer-finisher

C Monitor-evaluator

D Shaper **(2 marks)**

239 Which TWO of the following are key aspects of successful teams, as defined by Peters and Waterman?

A Teams should be relatively small.

B Membership of the team should be voluntary.

C Successful teams should be given a wide range of tasks in the long-term.

D There should be formal, well-structure communication channels within the team.

(2 marks)

MOTIVATING INDIVIDUALS AND GROUPS

240 Fimble Co is a large organisation with a range of incentives available to motivate and improve the performance of its staff. Which of the following incentives will be most appropriate for staff working in the HR department?

A Commission

B A bonus for each unit they produce (piece rate)

C Profit sharing

D Productivity plans **(2 marks)**

241 According to Herzberg, offering employees career progression and status increases within the organisation will improve their motivation.

Is this statement TRUE or FALSE?

A True

B False **(1 marks)**

242 Motivation refers to how hard you are willing to work whilst satisfaction refers to your contentment with your job.

Is this statement TRUE or FALSE?

A True

B False **(1 marks)**

243 Which of the following would best fit into Maslow's 'ego' category?

A Loss of one's home

B Winning an 'employee of the month' prize

C Challenging work

D Regular staff parties **(2 marks)**

244 Match the following statements with the level of Maslow's hierarchy of needs.

(i) A has been offered a large pay rise in recognition of his hard work on several recent projects.

(ii) B has been offered a permanent contract with the business she works for, giving her access to a good pension scheme.

(iii) C has been offered her first ever job with a company. The pay she receives will be sufficient to cover her essential costs.

A (i) – Basic, (ii) – Ego, (iii) – Security

B (i) – Self-fulfilment, (ii) – Basic, (iii) – Social

C (i) – Ego, (ii) – Security, (iii) – Basic

D (i) – Ego, (ii) – Social, (iii) – Security **(2 marks)**

245 **Anna manages a junior employee who has been performing very well in his job. Anna wishes to motivate him and has decided to offer him a greater level of responsibility within the business. What type of job redesign is Anna offering the junior employee?**

A Job enlargement

B Job rotation

C Job enrichment

D Job switching **(2 marks)**

246 **If you believe that you have Theory Y workers, which TWO of the following should a manager adopt?**

A An authoritarian style

B A participative style

C An emphasis on employee development **(1 mark)**

247 **According to Douglas McGregor, Theory X people are motivated by:**

A money and security

B achievement at work

C interpersonal relationships

D recognition for good work **(2 marks)**

248 'The absence of certain job features will reduce employee satisfaction. However, their presence will not result in positive motivation.'

What term relating to motivation does this refer to?

A Maslow's primary needs

B Herzberg hygiene factors

C McGregor Theory X

D Herzberg theory of job design **(2 marks)**

249 **Which one of the following is consistent with the 'ego' level of motivation within Maslow's hierarchy of needs?**

A Challenging job

B Sense of accomplishment

C Job title

D Job security **(2 marks)**

250 If a business operates a piecework system (where employees are paid for each unit they produce), it means that employees will need to be encouraged to ensure that the quality of their work is high.

Is this statement TRUE or FALSE?

A True

B False **(1 marks)**

LEARNING AND TRAINING AT WORK

251 A trainee accountant has been given a mentor at his/her firm. This mentor will be available to the student if he/she has any questions or needs further information about anything to do with their job.

This would be an example of ___________ learning for the trainee accountant.

Which word correctly fills the gap in the sentence above?

Incidental/formal/informal/self-managed*

*delete as appropriate **(2 marks)**

252 Learning can be defined as 'the process of acquiring knowledge through experience, which leads to a change ___________'.

Which word correctly completes this sentence?

A Perception

B Understanding

C Behaviour **(1 mark)**

253 Which TWO of the following are features of a 'learning organisation'?

(i) Learning from others and past experience

(ii) Avoidance of the risk of failure where possible

(iii) A detailed system of controls over employee activities

(iv) Generation and transfer of knowledge throughout the organisation

A (i) and (ii) only

B (i) and (iii) only

C (i) and (iv) only

D (ii) and (iv) only **(2 marks)**

254 Kolb has suggested that there are four stages in the learning process. Which is NOT one of these stages?

A Experience

B Active experimentation

C Observation and reflection

D Divergent **(2 marks)**

255 According to Honey and Mumford, what style of learning is being adopted by each person?

	Pragmatist	Reflector	Activist
J dislikes reading instruction booklets and prefers a hands-on approach to learning.			
H learns by watching others undertake a task first, before trying to imitate them.			

(2 marks)

256 Kolb argued that there are four stages to learning which always begins with concrete experience.

Is this statement TRUE or FALSE?

A True

B False **(1 marks)**

257 Accommodative learners enjoy concrete experiences and active experimentation.

Is this statement TRUE or FALSE?

A True

B False **(1 marks)**

258 Which of the following learning styles is best adjusted to acquiring knowledge from group interaction and team work?

A Activist

B Reflectors

C Theories

D Pragmatist **(2 marks)**

259 Honey and Mumford classified four different learning styles.

Which of the following statements accurately describes the pragmatist?

A Prefers to understand principles

B Prefers to think things through first

C Prefers to try things 'hands-on'

D Prefers to see practical examples **(2 marks)**

260 An important implication of Kolb and Honey and Mumford's theories is that people will tend to learn more effectively if:

A learning involves a significant amount of repetition

B learning is geared to their preferred learning style

C learning is supported by an enthusiastic teacher

D learning appears to offer tangible practical benefits **(2 marks)**

261 Which term matches each definition?

Definition	**Training**	**Education**	**Development**
'The activities which aim at developing skills, values and understanding required in all aspects of life.'			
'The growth or realisation of a person's ability and potential through conscious or unconscious learning.'			

(2 marks)

262 The following are the stages in the training and development process:

(i) Identification of needs

(ii) Evaluation and validation of the training programme

(iii) Programme design

(iv) Setting training objectives

In what order should these steps occur?

A (i), (iii), (ii), (iv)

B (iv), (i), (iii), (ii)

C (i), (iv), (iii), (ii)

D (iv), (ii), (iii), (i) **(2 marks)**

263 Alex is undertaking performance appraisal on his staff for the year. What stage in the training and development process would this be included within?

A Evaluation and validation

B Setting training objectives

C Identification of needs

D Programme design **(2 marks)**

REVIEW AND APPRAISAL OF INDIVIDUAL PERFORMANCE

264 Julian's manager has informed him of the goals that will be measured against for the coming year. At the end of the year, Julian's manager then discussed how well Julian performed against these targets in the year and what the following year's targets should be, along with how Julian would be expected to achieve this targets.

Which stage of the performance appraisal process is missing from Julian's appraisal?

A Monitor

B Review

C Action plan

D Set targets **(2 marks)**

265 Which of the following is NOT a usual purpose of annual performance appraisal?

A Deciding on remuneration levels for the coming period

B Decisions about whether to terminate an employee

C Identification of training and development needs

D Ensuring that work of particular merit is recognised **(2 marks)**

266 Performance assessment +criteria should only include quantitative issues, rather than skill or judgement-based criteria.

Is this statement TRUE or FALSE?

A True

B False **(1 mark)**

267 Performance appraisal could be seen as a part of a company's succession planning strategy.

Is this statement TRUE or FALSE?

A True

B False **(1 mark)**

268 Hans is an employee having an appraisal with his manager, Ali. Ali informs Hans that his performance has been poor throughout the year, giving a number of incidents and scenarios to back up her statements. She concludes that he needs additional training during the following year in order to improve his performance.

What type of appraisal has Hans had?

A Tell and sell

B Tell and listen

C Problem solving

D 360 degree **(2 marks)**

269 The reasons for staff leaving fall into three categories:

1 Discharge

2 Unavoidable

3 Avoidable

Which of the above options is/are correct?

A 1 and 2 only

B 1 and 3 only

C 2 and 3 only

D 1, 2 and 3 **(2 marks)**

270 Mary has recently been told that she is being dismissed from her job due to her no longer having the required skills for her role. Which of the following reasons for staff leaving would this be classified as?

A Discharge

B Avoidable

C Redundancy

D Unavoidable **(2 marks)**

271 Staff turnover can be calculated by dividing __________ by ___________ and expressing the result as a percentage.

1 The total number leaving the organisation

2 The total number in the workforce

3 The average number in the workforce

4 The weighted average number leaving the organisation

Which of the above options should be inserted into the gaps IN THE CORRECT ORDER to complete the calculation?

A 1 then 2

B 1 then 3

C 4 then 2

D 4 then 3 **(2 marks)**

272 Which of the following is not a key feature of effective appraisal?

A Firm

B Factual

C Frequent

D Formal **(2 marks)**

PERSONAL EFFECTIVENESS AT WORK

273 Violeta has a large number of tasks waiting for her attention and has realised she needs to prioritise them. One task is high importance but Violeta has a number of weeks left before the deadline for the task.

What approach should Violeta take to dealing with this task?

A Delegate or cancel the task

B Ignore the task completely

C Deal with the task now and devote plenty of time to it

D Delegate the task for now **(2 marks)**

274 Javier is struggling to manage his time effectively. Which of the following could be a reason for this?

A Javier has an established job with routine and predictable work

B Javier has his own office and operates a closed-door policy

C Javier's colleagues are all based in the same office as Javier

D Javier finds it difficult to be assertive with his colleagues **(2 marks)**

275 Consider the following two statements:

1 Intranets are designed to allow individuals to electronically send messages and attachments quickly and efficiently.

2 Electronic Data Interchange (EDI) enables automatic ordering between organisations, which reduces the need for physical goods request forms to be printed.

Which of these statements is/are correct?

A 1 only

B 2 only

C Both

D Neither **(2 marks)**

276 Which of the following statements regarding competency frameworks is incorrect?

A Competency frameworks can be used to identify training needs within the organisation

B Competency frameworks should be regularly updated for employees

C Competency frameworks are a list of the formal qualifications needed by anyone taking on a given role within the organisation **(1 mark)**

277 Counselling normally deals with issues such as:

1 a lack of experience or technical knowledge necessary to fulfil the job requirements.

2 the production of a set of concrete goals by the counsellor that the individual needs to achieve.

Which of these statements is/are correct?

A 1 only

B 2 only

C Both

D Neither **(2 marks)**

278 Which term matches each definition?

Definition	**Mentoring**	**Coaching**	**Counselling**
'The process of offering help, guidance and advice to facilitate the learning and development of another.'			
'Helping another individual to identify and deal with a problem or problems.'			

(2 marks)

279 Robert is a new employee at JKF Co. Olivia is a long-serving employee at JFK and has been asked to offer Robert any practical advice and support that he needs and act as a role model for Robert.

Olivia would therefore be classified as Robert's:

A Coach

B Mentor

C Counsellor

D Partner **(2 marks)**

280 Jennifer has a large number of work tasks that need doing in the near future. When deciding on which order to approach the tasks in, what should she consider?

A Her manager's suggestions

B Tasks with the highest business impact

C Do the easiest tasks first

D Do the most complex tasks first **(2 marks)**

281 Personal effectiveness is best described as:

A managing one's time efficiently

B achieving results quickly

C securing objectives without trampling on people

D setting the right goals and objectives and then securing them **(2 marks)**

282 Which of the following is NOT likely to be a goal of a personal development plan?

A Growth during a person's career

B Meeting weekly sales targets

C Developing skills and expertise

D Realising personal aspirations **(2 marks)**

283 Which TWO of the following are characteristics of good quality objectives?

1 Measurable

2 Time-constrained

3 Representative

4 Activity-based

A 1 and 2

B 2 and 4

C 2 and 3

D 1 and 3 **(2 marks)**

284 Two employees have recently been arguing over access to business computer systems. Their manager feels that the conflict is not serious and will sort itself out. Because of this, he/she has decided not to intervene. Which conflict management strategy is the manager adopting?

A Denial

B Suppression

C Reduction

D Resolution **(2 marks)**

285 Omar is a manager in BHB Co. Two of his employees are in conflict over access to key IT staff for their respective projects. Omar realises that the two managers have to work together regularly in the future but is worried that this serious conflict may destroy their working relationship. Omar has no control over access to IT staff.

Which approach to conflict management would be the most appropriate for Omar to adopt?

A Resolution

B Suppression

C Denial

D Reduction **(2 marks)**

286 Samantha is concerned that a member of her staff is not performing effectively at work.

Which of the following could be a consequence of the staff member's ineffectiveness?

A Loss of reputation and customers

B Reduced need for employee training

C Increased staff motivation

D A rise in productivity **(2 marks)**

COMMUNICATING IN BUSINESS

287 Consider the following statements:

1 The grapevine communication network is often used by managers to pass on orders and instruction to staff.

2 When communicating with others, the majority of information passed on to the other person is transmitted through words rather than other means such as body language or tone of voice.

Which of these statements is/are correct?

A 1 only

B 2 only

C Both

D Neither **(2 marks)**

288 The use of predetermined lists of recipients for instructions, control reports, etc. often results in some of the recipients investigating matters which have no relevance to the job they do.

Is this statement TRUE or FALSE?

A True

B False **(1 mark)**

289 Barriers to communication consist of anything that stops information getting to its intended recipients.

Is this statement TRUE or FALSE?

A True

B False **(1 mark)**

290 Which of the following is an example of lateral communication?

A A manager explaining new operational procedures to staff

B A committee coming together to review health and safety issues

C Staff passing on to the supervisor the main points from a recent conversation with a customer

D During appraisal, a person receives feedback about their performance results

(2 marks)

291 Indira is a manager in A Co. Her employees have recently complained that I's department is suffering from a lack of upwards communication. Which of the following problems would typically result from this?

A Divisions between the management team

B Lack of co-ordination

C Limited participation in decision-making by junior staff

D Lack of awareness of corporate objectives by more junior employees **(2 marks)**

292 Felix has recently sent out an email informing his colleagues of a change to an order placed by one of their major customers. His colleagues are now complaining that they have already started work on the customer order and this work has now been wasted.

What attribute of effective communication is missing from Felix's communication?

A Complete

B Cost-effective

C Relevant

D Timely **(2 marks)**

293 Information overload usually leads to individuals being unable to decide what information is relevant or not, and therefore important facts may be missed out.

Is this statement TRUE or FALSE?

A True

B False **(1 mark)**

294 Research on communication networks has shown that the quickest way to reach a conclusion is always through:

A the Circle

B the 'Y'

C the wheel

D the chain **(2 marks)**

295 Under time pressure, the all-channels system:

A delivers even better results

B reforms into a circle or disintegrates

C slows down or crashes

D restructures or disintegrates **(2 marks)**

296 For complex problems the network most likely to facilitate the best decision is:

A circle

B all-channel

C wheel

D 'Y' **(2 marks)**

297 Which of the following statements is an example of diagonal communication?

A A junior accountant communicating with the finance director

B A team leader communicating with another team leader in a different department

C A junior marketing manager communicating with the procurement manager

D The finance director communicating with the sales director **(2 marks)**

298 Hugo manages a team in GSA Co. He emails information to individual team members as needed. The team members send information back to Hugo and then he forwards any relevant points out to the rest of the team. Individual team members do not communicate with each other.

Which type of communication network is Hugo's team operating?

A Y

B Wheel

C Circle

D All channel **(2 marks)**

Section 2

MULTI-TASK QUESTIONS – SECTION B

THE BUSINESS ORGANISATION AND ITS EXTERNAL ENVIRONMENT

1 (a) F Co is attempting to classify its stakeholders.

Classify the following stakeholders as either internal or connected.

Stakeholder	Internal	Connected
Employees		
Shareholders		
Customers		
Directors		

(0.5 marks each = 2 marks total)

(b) F Co wishes to use Mendelow's matrix to decide on what approach to take to each stakeholder.

The following sentences contain gaps which specify which approach to stakeholder management should be taken.

F Co is partly owned by H, who is considered to have high power and low interest. F Co has therefore decided to use a _1_ strategy to manage this stakeholder.

(i) Select the type of approach from Mendelow's matrix that appropriately fills gap 1 above.

Keep informed/Key players/Keep satisfied/Minimal effort*

*delete as appropriate

F Co is aware that its actions are regularly commented on by HHH, which would be classified by Mendelow as _2_. HHH has a high level of interest, but low power.

(ii) Select the type of approach from Mendelow's matrix that appropriately fills gap 2 above.

Keep informed/Key players/Keep satisfied/Minimal effort*

*delete as appropriate **(1 mark each = 2 marks in total)**

(Total: 4 marks)

2 FFD Co is a large national manufacturer of animal feed based in country T. FFD sells dried food – primarily for chickens and sheep. This is not a competitive market and FFD's large number of small farmer customers have little alternative but to purchase FFD's products for their animals. The farming industry is struggling in country T with farmers earning very low margins and many being forced out of business.

The Government of country T has publicly expressed concerns about the state of the national farming industry and has vowed to do whatever is necessary to protect farmers from what one minister has referred to as 'money-making corporations that are making excessive profits from farmers.'

FFD's shares are mainly held by individual investors – many of whom have invested a significant amount of money into FFD. No one shareholder in FFD has more than 4% of the total share capital of the company.

FFD's employees are largely unskilled and are not members of any union.

FFD is currently considering raising its prices by around 15% to improve its margins. It has identified four main stakeholder groups who may be affected by the decision. These have been allocated to the quadrants in the matrix shown below.

		Stakeholder interest	
		High	**Low**
Stakeholder power	**High**	A	B
	Low	C	D

Indicate which quadrant of the matrix each stakeholder group has been allocated to.

Stakeholder	**A**	**B**	**C**	**D**
Customers				
Government				
Shareholders				
Employees				

(1 mark each, total = 4 marks)

(Total: 4 marks)

3 (a) PH is a company that runs train services between several major cities in country B. It is currently undertaking a strategic planning exercise for its future operations and has decided to analyse its external environment using a PEST analysis.

This analysis has uncovered a number of major issues within Country B that PH needs to plan for.

Which FOUR of the following statements would be most likely to be classified as 'Political' factors within a PEST analysis?

A Country B's government has announced additional expenditure on motorways and roads

B Residents of country B are becoming more environmentally conscious

C New internet systems are available that will simplify the process of booking train tickets

D New health and safety regulations are being planned for all rail operators in country B

E Increased congestion on the roads of country B as residents travel more

F Additional one-off taxes on rail operators are being proposed in country B to help pay for road upgrades

G Rise in the cost of repairs to trains due to a shortage of skilled labour in country B

H Government-mandated regulation are being introduced to enforce targets for on-time train arrivals and departures **(0.5 marks each, total = 2 marks)**

(b) Economies can suffer from several different types of inflation, including:

A Expectations

B Monetary

C Imported

D Demand-pull

Classify the following as relating to either A (expectations), B (monetary), C (imported) or D (demand-pull):

(i) Employees in Country F are demanding a 5% pay rise to ensure that they will be no worse off after the predicted rate of inflation for the coming year.

(ii) Sales of smart-phones are booming in country F, leading to price rises.

(iii) Country F's currency has weakened, leading to rises in the costs of oil purchased from abroad.

(iv) Country F's Government has increased the money supply through quantitative easing.

(0.5 marks each = 2 marks total)

(Total: 4 marks)

4 (a) BVO is a small business, which manufactures and sells a number of products, including product X (a relatively low-value item). BVO has recently been considering its pricing policy for this product.

It has estimated that if it raises the current selling price (per unit) of product X from $1 to $1.50, annual demand will drop from 100,000 units to 90,000 units.

BVO is uncertain of the implications of this for its product, or what might be causing the current level of price elasticity.

Which FOUR of the following options could reasonably be inferred from the above information?

A The price elasticity of demand (PED) for product X is 5

B Product X is unit elastic

C Product X may be a product that customers buy out of habit

D Product X may have few, if any, substitutes

E The price elasticity of demand (PED) for product X is 0.28

F Product X may see a sharper fall in demand if the price rise lasts for a long period.

G Product X has a price elasticity of demand (PED) of 0.2

H Product X would be more profitable if the price was cut rather than raised

(0.5 marks each, total = 2 marks)

(b) The following sentences contain gaps which are missing a particular micro-economic term.

BVO has noted that product Y's sales have fallen in recent years due to a fall in disposable income of its major customers. This is evidence that _1_ in the demand curve for the product has occurred.

(i) Select the term, from the following list, that appropriately fills gap 1 above.

a shift/a duopoly/equilibrium/a contraction*

*delete as appropriate

BVO sells product Z in country G. Only one other manufacturer sells a similar product in country G, meaning that the two companies dominate the market. Currently, production and sales volumes for these products has reached exactly the same levels, suggesting _2_ in the market for this product.

(ii) Select the term, from the following list, that appropriately fills gap 2 above.

a shift/a duopoly/equilibrium/a contraction*

*delete as appropriate **(1 mark each = 2 marks in total)**

(Total: 4 marks)

5 (a) Y Co sells health and home insurance. Y does not have any physical stores – instead it has a number of call centres. Customers make contact with the company and purchase insurance policies over the phone.

Y's call centre management structure is extremely bureaucratic, with many levels of management. This results in Y suffering high payroll costs, leading to it having to increase its prices to customers, reducing its ability to compete in the insurance market.

However, Y has recently started to introduce new computerised systems for its call centre staff, which has led to increased efficiency. Staff members are able to deal with significantly more calls than previously and less skill is required by the employees, as much of the complex work is now undertaken by the new system.

Y is now looking to see what changes it can make to the call centres as a result of introducing the new IT system. It is considering three options.

Classify the following issues as relating to either delayering, downsizing or outsourcing.

Issue	**Delayering**	**Downsizing**	**Outsourcing**
Could allow third party organisations access to Y's information and processes, leading to loss of competitive advantage.			
Keeping the current management structure, but reducing the number of staff could lead to demotivation among the remaining workers.			
Eliminating several levels of unnecessary management to reduce Y's costs, leading to lower prices for customers.			
This is likely to lead to a more 'team-working' approach, where employees take on different roles in different teams, as necessary.			

(0.5 marks each = 2 marks total)

(b) Y has decided to examine the idea of outsourcing its functions in more detail. Y's management team have been told that there are four distinct types of outsourcing.

The following sentences contain gaps which specify a particular type of outsourcing.

Y is considering outsourcing some of its call centre activities to GH Co. GH will provide _1_ outsourcing, with GH operators taking calls from new customers looking to purchase a policy. Y's existing staff will deal with existing customer renewals, queries and complaints.

(i) Select the type of outsourcing that appropriately fills gap 1 above.

total/project management/ad hoc/partial*

*delete as appropriate

Y has been approached by another company, HG Co, which has offered to provide extra call centre staff in the month of January – which is the busiest time of year for Y. This _2_ outsourcing would help Y to avoid losing customers due to the long delays customers can face on the phone during this month.

(ii) Select the type of outsourcing that appropriately fills gap 2 above.

total/project management/ad hoc/partial*

*delete as appropriate **(1 mark each = 2 marks in total)**

(Total: 4 marks)

6 MBV is a manufacturer of fine furniture based in country G. MBV's managers have identified that the company's results for the past three years have been declining. They feel that this is due to changes in the external environment – in particular within MBV's industry.

The managers wish to use Porter's five forces model to understand the problems the company is facing, but are uncertain of its proper use. They have undertaken some analysis and identified a number of key issues (summarised below) but cannot decide which of the five forces each issue relates to.

		Level	
		High	**Low**
	New entrants	A	B
	Power of buyers	C	D
Force	**Power of suppliers**	E	F
	Power of rivals	G	H
	Substitutes	I	J

For EACH of the following issues, identify which force they relate to and whether the strength of the force is high or low, by choosing ONE letter from A to J.

Issue	A	B	C	D	E	F	G	H	I	J
MBV's employees are heavily unionised, making it difficult for the company to change their terms and conditions.										
MBV's products are sold through two main retail chains in country G. Each retailer sells approximately equal amounts of MBV's furniture.										
MBV is much larger than any other fine furniture manufacturers in country G, which has given it an advantage due to significant economies of scale. MBV still retails its products at a similar price to its rivals.										
The market for fine furniture in country G is growing very slowly.										

(1 mark each, total = 4 marks)

(Total: 4 marks)

7 (a) Here are four short references to activities within Porter's value chain:

A Storing and handling inputs

B Activities after the point of sale

C The way the business is organised

D Purchasing of all inputs, including materials

Identify the description above, which is associated with EACH of the following value chain activities, by matching them up with A, B, C, D or None.

(i) Inbound logistics

(ii) Procurement

(iii) Service

(iv) Operations

(v) Infrastructure **(0.5 marks each, total = 2.5 marks)**

(b) **Which THREE of the following statements, regarding Porter's generic strategies, are correct?**

A Focus involves offering general goods to a small segment of the market at a low price

B Cost leadership involves manufacturing goods more efficiently than rivals

C Businesses may become cost leaders by making their goods a lower quality than their rivals

D A focus strategy tends to allow businesses to charge a premium price

E Differentiation involves charging a premium for a product due to its actual or perceived benefits to the customer

F Businesses that are stuck in the middle are trying to sell products at too high a price. **(0.5 marks each, total = 1.5 marks)**

(Total: 4 marks)

8 (a) **Identify the type of unemployment above which is associated with each of the following descriptions.**

	Cyclical	**Real wage**	**Structural**	**Frictional**
Tends to occur in industries that are highly unionised.				
Caused by aggregate demand in the economy being too low to create employment opportunities.				
Short-term unemployment as people move between jobs.				
Caused by changes in the skills required by the economy.				

(0.5 marks each, total = 2 marks)

(b) The following sentences contain gaps which are missing a particular economic term.

Management of the Government's taxation and spending plans is known as _1_.

(i) Select the term that appropriately fills gap 1 above.

deflationary gap/fiscal policy/monetary policy/stagflation*

*delete as appropriate

Poor economic growth over an extended period can sometimes lead to rises in the prices of goods and services. This is referred to as _2_.

(ii) Select the term that appropriately fills gap 2 above.

deflationary gap/fiscal policy/monetary policy/stagflation*

*delete as appropriate **(1 mark each = 2 marks in total)**

(Total: 4 marks)

9 POL bottles and sells natural spring water in country H. It is the best-selling brand of bottled water in country H and has a highly recognisable brand name. POL is long-established and has a very experienced management team. Many years of high profits have enabled the company to build up significant cash reserves.

The market for bottled water has been slow-growing for many years in country H, with consumers switching to flavoured waters, which are not offered by POL. Nearby country I (which POL does not currently operate in) is seeing significant growth in this market.

One of POL's managers has recently noted an article in a popular newspaper in country H which suggested that bottled water may be harmful to health due to high levels of toxins from the plastic bottles the water is sold in. POL is one of the few bottled water manufacturers to sell its water in glass bottles, which the article suggests is safe for consumption.

One of POL's successful smaller competitors, AQA, has recently been put up for sale by its owners who wish to exit country H. POL's management team is considering making an offer for the company in order to increase their market share in country H.

(a) Below are some key issues which POL's managers have identified as part of a SWOT analysis.

Which FOUR of the following are issues that are most likely to be classified as opportunities for POL, based on the above information.

A Expansion into bottled water sales in country I

B Potential health risks from plastic bottles

C Strong cash balances

D Launch of new flavoured waters in country H

E Experienced managers

F Strong brand name

G Potential purchase of AQA

H Slow growth in the bottled water market in country H

(0.5 marks each, total = 2 marks)

(b) In order to improve margins, POL has decided to undertake a value chain analysis of the company's existing water bottling operations.

Identify the activity from the value chain model which is associated with each of the following descriptions.

	Operations	Outbound logistics	Service	Procurement
POL has a small call centre dedicated to dealing with customer complaints.				
Water is filtered through a four-stage process before being purified and bottled.				
POL's purchasing department regularly shops around to get the lowest possible price for POL's glass bottles from suppliers.				
Bottled water is held in large warehouses before being transported to retailers across country H.				

(0.5 marks each, total = 2 marks)

(Total: 4 marks)

ORGANISATIONAL STRUCTURE, CULTURE, GOVERNANCE AND SUSTAINABILITY

10 (a) Modern structural theory includes 'boundaryless' organisations.

Classify the following as relating to either hollow, virtual or modular.

	Hollow	Virtual	Modular
Internal functions that give competitive advantage to the company are outsourced to third parties.			
The manufacturing of some components of the company's product are outsourced to third parties.			
Only non-core functions are outsourced to third parties.			
The organisation only exists as a network of contracts.			

(0.5 marks each = 2 marks total)

(b) W Co is a bank and has many stakeholders – including many different types of organisation.

The following sentences contain gaps which specify a particular type of organisation.

W Co is partly owned by Z, a _1_ that has recently sold a large number of its shares on the open market in order to raise finance.

(i) Select the type of organisation that appropriately fills gap 1 above.

non-governmental organisation/public limited company/private limited company/public organisation*

*delete as appropriate

W Co is aware that its actions are regularly commented on by VVV, which is a _2_. VVV campaigns for fair banking and has recently been granted charitable status.

(ii) Select the type of organisation that appropriately fills gap 2 above.

non-governmental organisation/public limited company/private limited company/public organisation*

*delete as appropriate **(1 mark each = 2 marks in total)**

(Total: 4 marks)

11 (a) PASS is a small business which trains accountancy students in a number of small offices across country C. Each office is headed by a manager.

PASS's management team is considering the launch of several new strategies for the organisation, but one of the managers has stated that he/she is unsure which of the three levels of strategy each one relates to.

Classify each of the following strategies as relating to strategic, operational or tactical planning levels.

	Strategic	Operational	Tactical
PASS's office managers have started detailed planning of shift patterns for all PASS tutors.			
PASS is considering the acquisition of a small, rival training company.			
PASS's managers are considering offering human resource management courses as well as accountancy training.			
PASS's managers have decided to increase the number of staff in one particular PASS office.			

(0.5 marks each, total = 2 marks)

(b) PASS currently has an entrepreneurial structure, with one main owner-manager (Mr F) to whom all of PASS's managers report directly.

Mr F is considering restructuring the organisation and moving to a functional structure.

Which FOUR of the following statements are the most likely potential benefits of PASS moving to a functional structure?

A Strategic decisions will be made more quickly

B Conflict between functions will be reduced

C The new structure will lead to duplication of roles

D It will increase PASS's ability to expand

E It will enable PASS to maximise its access to economies of scale

F The new structure will increase standardisation of PASS's products

G Increased local decision making

H Career opportunities for staff will be enhanced

(0.5 marks each, total = 2 marks)

(Total: 4 marks)

12 GRR makes soft toy animals for children, which are sold through a number of toy stores. GRR has made losses for the last two years and feels it may be due to problems with its basic marketing mix.

(a) Below are some key ideas which GRR's managers have identified as part of a basic marketing mix analysis.

Which four of the following issues would be most likely to be classified as PRODUCT issues with GRR's marketing mix?

A Discounts offered to customers who buy three or more toys at the same time

B New, brighter packaging on all toys

C Toys to be made 25% larger than currently

D Sale of toys directly to customers through GRR's website

E Improved after-sale care to customers, following complaints by customers

F Provision of a 2-year warranty on all toys sold

G Reduction in price of all products by 15%

H New advertisements for key products in national newspapers

(0.5 marks each, total = 2 marks)

(b) GRR is considering its pricing strategies for a new range of stuffed dinosaur toys.

Identify the pricing strategy which is most closely associated with each of the following descriptions.

	Penetration pricing	Going rate pricing	Cost plus pricing	Price skimming
The toys could be launched at a low initial price to gain market share and then the price is raised later to maximise profits.				
The toys are fairly innovative, so GRR may launch them at a high price and then drop them to a lower level later when its rivals launch similar products.				
GRR may sell its toys at the same price as similar rival products to ensure it is able to compete successfully.				
GRR could sell the products at a 15% mark-up.				

(0.5 marks each, total = 2 marks)

(Total: 4 marks)

13 G is a multinational company that provides IT support to its clients.

It is aware that there are significant cultural differences between its operations in different countries. G's managers have decided to undertake an analysis of its corporate culture in each of its countries of operations using Hofstede's cultural dimensions.

	Level	
<u>Dimension</u>	**High**	**Low**
Individualism	A	B
Uncertainty avoidance	C	D
Power distance	E	F
Motivation towards achievement and success	G	H
Long-term orientation	I	J
Indulgence	K	L

For EACH of the following issues, identify which dimension they relate to and whether they indicate that this dimension is high or low by selecting ONE letter from A to L.

(i) **Staff members in country A expect to have significant input into the design of their jobs, as well as the decision-making process.**

A/B/C/D/E/F/G/H/I/J/K/L*

*select one

(ii) **Employees in country B have very strict social norms on a range of issues such as dress, behaviour and language.**

A/B/C/D/E/F/G/H/I/J/K/L*

*select one

(iii) **Staff in country C are motivated by pay rises and new job titles.**

A/B/C/D/E/F/G/H/I/J/K/L*

*select one

(iv) **Employees in country D prefer a bureaucratic management style with rules and procedures to ensure mistakes are minimised.**

A/B/C/D/E/F/G/H/I/J/K/L*

*select one **(1 mark each, total = 4 marks)**

(Total: 4 marks)

14 (a) Handy identified four cultural types.

Identify which culture is associated with each of the following descriptions.

	Power	Person	Task	Role
Typically a bureaucratic organisation.				
Often found in owner-managed organisations.				
The culture exists to satisfy the needs of particular individuals.				
People usually describe their position in terms of the results they are achieving.				

(0.5 marks each, total = 2 marks)

(b) **Which FOUR of the following statements, regarding culture, are consistent with Edgar Schein's cultural analysis?**

A Culture is usually defined by the organisation's first leaders

B Culture is 'the way we do things round here'

C Basic assumptions and values are unseen and difficult to identify

D Espoused values are the aspects of culture that are easy to identify

E Norms guide people's behaviour within the organisation

F An example of 'artefacts' could be corporate dress codes

G Schein examined differences between cultures in different countries

H Espoused values could include the organisation's stated goals

(0.5 marks each, total = 2 marks)

(Total: 4 marks)

15 (a) C Co has a number of key committees, as recommended by relevant codes of corporate governance.

Are the following statements true or false?

Statement	**True**	**False**
Audit committees are responsible for reviewing accounting policies and ensuring they are appropriate.		
Remuneration committees should be made up of two or more non-executive directors if the company is small.		
The nominations committee helps the company to select which of the nominated audit firms should be selected by the company.		
Both internal and external auditors report to the audit committee.		

(0.5 marks each, total = 2 marks)

(b) **Which FOUR of the following statements are correct with regards to committees.**

A Ad hoc committees are formed for a particular purpose on a permanent basis

B Committees can be used a delaying mechanism

C Committees are often slow at making decisions due to internal disagreements

D The Chairperson is typically responsible for preparing the minutes of meetings

E The Secretary is typically responsible for ensuring the meeting is kept on time

F Committees make decisions that are often more easily accepted by the organisation

G Committees enjoy collective responsibility

H Standing committees are typically temporary in nature

(0.5 marks each, total = 2 marks)

(Total: 4 marks)

16 (a) L Co has recently decided to convert to a public company in order to sell its shares on its local stock exchange. It is concerned that it lacks the appropriate knowledge of the corporate governance requirements that are typically required when seeking a listing.

Which FOUR of the following statements regarding best practise relating to non-executive directors (NEDs) are correct?

A NEDs have no day-to-day managerial responsibilities

B Best practise suggests that NEDs should not serve with the same company for more than five years

C NEDs should not take share options in the company, but can participate in its pension scheme

D NEDs attend board meetings and have a say in the strategic decision-making of the company

E Smaller companies should have at least two NEDs on their board

F NEDs should never have had a material business interest in the company they are working for

G NEDs shouldn't have any close links to the executive directors

(0.5 marks each, total = 2 marks)

(b) L has also been made aware of a number of committees that they will be expected to form if they seek a listing.

The following sentences are extracts from this report, but they have gaps where the name of the relevant committee has been omitted.

'The _1_ committee is responsible for ensuring that there is an appropriate mix of skills and experience on the board, as well as making sure there are sufficient non-executive directors.'

(i) Select the term that appropriately fills gap 1 above.

remuneration/audit/nomination/public oversight*

*delete as appropriate

'Wholly staffed by non-executive directors, the _2_ committee reviews systems of internal control as well as reviewing the accounting policies of the company.'

(ii) Select the term that appropriately fills gap 2 above.

remuneration/audit/nomination/public oversight*

*delete as appropriate **(1 mark each = 2 marks in total)**

(Total: 4 marks)

BUSINESS FUNCTIONS, REGULATION AND TECHNOLOGY

17 (a) PPR is a supermarket which is developing a new information system for its managers.

Identify which of the following statements relate to the information that would typically be produced by strategic information systems or operational information systems.

Information	Strategic	Operational
Long-term focus		
Highly detailed		
Produced frequently		
Mainly an internal focus		

(0.5 marks each, total = 2 marks)

(b) PPR's Information Manager (IM) has identified four major types of information system that the company may wish to adopt.

The following sentences from PPR's IM report contain gaps.

'PPR has a till system which records each sale made through the day. At the end of the day, this _1_ summarises all the information on sales for the day and produces a report.'

(i) **Select the term that appropriately fills gap 1 above.**

management information system/expert system/transaction processing system/decision support system*

*delete as appropriate

'PPR's _2_ enables us to quickly calculate our tax bill for the year. We have complex rules we need to follow with this calculation and they are all pre-programmed into this system.'

(ii) **Select the term that appropriately fills gap 2 above.**

management information system/expert system/transaction processing system/decision support system*

*delete as appropriate **(1 mark each = 2 marks in total)**

(Total: 4 marks)

18 (a) Y Co has recently prepared its most recent set of financial statements. A newly appointed finance junior has pointed out a number of issues with the financial statements, which he/she has argued indicate that the statements are not true and fair.

Which FOUR of the above statements would make Y's financial statements no longer true and fair?

A Inventory was not valued using standard generally accepted practice.

B The financial statements used terminology that the junior felt would not be understood by the general public.

C Information was not sufficiently detailed – liabilities were not split out into their constituent elements.

D Y's receivables balance was slightly misstated, though Y acknowledged it would not affect the overall view of Y's performance by users.

E The layout of Y's cash flow statement was not in accordance with the relevant accounting standard.

F The financial statements covered 12 months – the previous set of financial statements covered 15 months.

G The cash balance was significantly misstated, meaning that it gave a misleading view of the financial position of the company.

(0.5 marks each, total = 2 marks)

(b) Y's junior accountant has been asked to produce a briefing note to her employers that covers the roles of the main accountancy standard-setting organisations, including:

A International Accounting Standards Board (IASB)

B IFRS Interpretations Committee (IFRS IC)

C IFRS Advisory Councils (IFRS AC)

D IFRS Foundation

However, the junior accountant is unsure of which roles are undertaken by each of these bodies.

Identify which of the following statements relate to the either the IASB, the IFRS IC, the IFRS AC or the IFRS Foundation by matching each of them to a letter A, B, C or D.

(i) Reviews widespread accounting issues and provides guidance.

(ii) Comprised of a wide range of members affected by the work of the other two bodies.

(iii) Development and publication of IFRSs and interpretations.

(iv) Acts as supervisory body for the other three bodies and ensures each is properly funded. **(0.5 marks each, total = 2 marks)**

(Total: 4 marks)

19 (a) K Co has recently split its accounting function into two parts – one that deals with management accounting and the other with financial accounting.

Identify which of the following statements relate to management accounting or financial accounting.

	Management accounting	**Financial accounting**
Preparation of the statement of profit or loss		
Recording of business transactions		
Preparation of statements for K Co's internal use		
No legal formats used		

(0.5 marks each, total = 2 marks)

(b) K's treasury function has released a report into a number of key finance areas.

Complete the following sentences from K's treasury department report.

(i) 'Debt/equity* is the best way of raising external finance for K, as it never has to be repaid by the company.'

*delete as appropriate

(ii) 'K has recently entered into a scheme that will reduce its tax bill significantly. It is believed that, while legal, it is designed to defeat the tax laws laid down by the Government. As such, it is classified as a tax mitigation/tax avoidance* scheme.'

*delete as appropriate **(1 mark each = 2 marks in total)**

(Total: 4 marks)

20 (a) GBF is a small, newly formed company that is preparing its annual financial statements for the first time. GBF is owned and run by one person, Juliette. She has limited financial knowledge and has therefore employed a firm of chartered accountants to produce the financial statements for her. J's accountants have now sent her a set of financial statements, which includes GBF's:

Juliette has a list of figures that one of her friends told her she should try and find from the financial statements, but she is uncertain.

Identify which of the following figures could be found, or calculated from the statement of profit or loss (SOPL), the statement of financial position (SOFP) or the statement of cash flows (SOCF).

	SOPL	SOFP	SOCF
Shareholders' equity			
Total cash spent purchasing non-current assets			
Gross margin			
Administrative expenses			

(0.5 marks each, total = 2 marks)

(b) Juliette was also told by her accountants that she should consider undertaking a number of internal management accounting functions to help her make important business decisions for the company.

The accountants suggested she needed to:

A Estimate GBF's total income and costs for the coming year to help her identify any opportunities or threats to the business

B Compare her expected results to her actual results at the end of the year to identify any areas GBF needs to improve on

C Calculate the cost per unit for GBF's products to help decide on appropriate pricing strategies

D Estimate the level of overdraft that GBF will need each month for the coming year

Match up EACH of the descriptions above (A, B, C and D) with its associated management accounting report below.

(i) Cash budget

(ii) Variance report

(iii) Standard cost card

(iv) Profit and loss budget **(0.5 marks each, total = 2 marks)**

(Total: 4 marks)

21 (a) TGD offers life insurance through a team of door-to-door salesmen in country P. This is a highly regulated industry in country P – the salesmen must ask specific questions and make specific statements to ensure that the policies they sell are legally binding. Any failure to do this can void the insurance policy and could in some cases lead to prosecution of TGD by the Government of country P. TGD has regular audits of its practices and records by the Government.

Currently TGD relies on a training programme for its salesmen which teaches them the rules and regulations they have to follow. However, in recent months TGD has discovered that a number of policies have been sold without all of the appropriate rules being followed. TGD is therefore considering the launch of a series of formal procedures that all salesmen must follow. This will be written into a set of documents that the salesman must go through with the customer to ensure that all legal requirements have been met.

Which FOUR of the following statements are consistent with TGD's proposed shift to a set of formal procedure?

A Slower training for new salesmen.

B Sales staff have formal documents to refer to if they are in doubt as to the correct procedure.

C Easier for Government auditors to check TGD's compliance with appropriate regulations.

D Reduced risk of fines and legal action by the Government.

E Cases where the correct procedures have not been followed are easier to identify.

F It will improve the ease with which salesmen can deal with non-standard transactions.

G It reduces TGD's overall cost of administration.

H It allows all transactions to be recorded in different ways, increasing flexibility.

(0.5 marks each = 2 marks total)

(b) TGD's managers are also examining their purchasing system and have identified the following stages:

A Ordering

B Goods received

C Requisition

D Invoice recorded

Place the stages into the correct order, beginning with the earliest.

(0.5 marks each, total = 2 marks)

(Total: 4 marks)

22 (a) PDP makes and sells computer monitors. It is considering the introduction of a number of controls during the next year, including:

A Authorisation of timesheets

B Bank reconciliations

C Checking creditworthiness of customers

D Agreeing goods received notes to invoices received

Match up EACH of the controls above with ONE of the following systems within PDP.

(i) Purchases system

(ii) Sales system

(iii) Cash system

(iv) Payroll system **(0.5 marks each, total = 2 marks)**

(b) PDP has an internal audit department whose main focus is to monitor the internal controls that have been implemented within the business. Below are a number of statements regarding internal audit.

Which FOUR of the following statements are correct?

A Internal audit is an independent appraisal activity

B Internal audit is carried out solely for the benefit of the organisation's shareholders

C The internal audit function should ideally report directly to the Audit Committee/ Board of Directors

D Internal auditors are appointed by the Audit Committee/ Board of Directors

E The scope of the internal auditors' work is prescribed by legislation

F The need for internal audit depends entirely on the number of employees within the organisation

G The internal audit department should not get involved with operational matters

H The internal audit function provides reasonable assurance as to whether the financial statements are free from material misstatement

(0.5 marks each, total = 2 marks)

(Total: 4 marks)

23 (a) **Which FOUR of the following statements are components of an internal control system?**

A Control environment

B Corrective

C Monitoring

D Risk assessment

E Application

F Information systems

G General

H Management responsibility **(0.5 marks each, total = 2 marks)**

(b) **Which FOUR of the following statements relate to internal audit?**

A It is a legal requirement for larger companies

B The scope of work is decided by management

C Can be undertaken by employees of the company

D Ultimately reports to the company's shareholders

E Reviews whether financial statements are true and fair

F Must be undertaken by independent auditors

G Mainly focuses on reviewing internal controls

H Ultimately reports to management **(0.5 marks each, total = 2 marks)**

(Total: 4 marks)

24 (a) BFG is a busy doctors' surgery. It has a complex information technology system which it uses to record patient details.

The information contained on BFG's information system must be accurate. Any errors in patient details or records could lead to inaccurate medical support which could seriously compromise patient health and wellbeing.

BFG has therefore decided to implement a number of controls over its patient records system.

Which FOUR of the following statements are general controls?

A All computer terminals are to be located in parts of the building that have code entry systems to limit unauthorised access.

B Off-site backups are to be kept of all patient records

C Automated checks that all patient records have been completed with all necessary data will be enforced

D Unique identification numbers will be issued for all users, allowing each piece of data input to be traced to a relevant staff member

E Training for all staff members in the correct use of the system will be put in place

F Authorisation controls will be enacted so that employees can only input information on the system that they are entitled to input or amend

G Password systems on all terminals will be created

H Validity checks will be made on data entered, such as age and height of patients

(0.5 marks each = 2 marks total)

(b) BFG's Office Manager has recently attended a lecture on the components of internal control.

The following are extracts from a report that BFG's Office Manager has sent to his/her colleagues. The extracts contain gaps.

'For BFG, I have concerns about our _1_, as the senior managers take little notice of our control systems and don't seem to see them as important.'

(i) Select the term that appropriately fills gap 1 above.

control activities/control environment/risk assessment processes/monitoring of controls*

*delete as appropriate

'There are some areas where we lack appropriate _2_. In particular we need segregation of duties when dealing with cash receipts.'

(ii) Select the term that appropriately fills gap 2 above.

control activities/control environment/risk assessment processes/monitoring of controls*

*delete as appropriate **(1 mark each = 2 marks in total)**

(Total: 4 marks)

25 (a) Here are four short references to possible frauds faced by organisations:

A Receipts from one debtor are taken by the fraudster, who then uses receipts from another debtor to clear this sales ledger balance

B The fraudster diverts small amounts from a large number of transactions

C A company is asked to pay a small amount up front in order to secure a larger later payment

D A fake investment is created, where high investment returns are paid to early investors out of the investments made by subsequent investors

Match up EACH of the descriptions above with ONE of the following frauds.

(i) Ponzi scheme

(ii) Teeming and lading

(iii) Skimming

(iv) Advance fee fraud **(0.5 marks each, total = 2 marks)**

(b) One serious type of fraud is money laundering.

The following sentences contain gaps relating to key money laundering terms.

'_1_ involves transferring money between businesses or locations in order to conceal their original source.'

(i) Select the term that appropriately fills gap 1 above.

layering/tipping off/placement/integration*

*delete as appropriate

'Recently, a criminal used stolen cash to buy shares in a company. This is an example of _2_.'

(ii) Select the type of organisation that appropriately fills gap 2 above.

layering/tipping off/placement/integration*

*delete as appropriate **(1 mark each = 2 marks in total)**

(Total: 4 marks)

26 (a) BBX Co is a small company that manufactures bicycles. It has a small accounts department with one main bookkeeper (Mr E) and two assistants. The owners of BBX have recently identified a number of factors relating to the accounts department that they feel could suggest that fraudulent activity is taking place.

Which FOUR of the following statements are most likely to indicate an increased risk of fraud in BBX?

A Mr E is well paid and happy in his current role

B Opening and recording cash receipts is always done by Mr E and one other, rotating member of staff

C The accounts department is dominated by Mr E – he is the only member of the accounts staff who is in the office full time

D Mr E has recently moved to a large house in an expensive part of the local area

E BBX's senior management rarely investigate or query any part of the financial statements or budgets for the company

F BBX has significant internal controls which are regularly checked by external auditors

G Mr E takes similar holidays each year

H BBX's managers have noted that payments to suppliers were far higher than anticipated over the last year and have been unable to explain this

(0.5 marks each = 2 marks total)

(b) YYT is a large company that is listed on its local stock exchange. Just like BBX, it is concerned that there may be fraud within its accounts department. One of the directors has suggested that YYT has not been effective at combating fraud because it is confused about who has the responsibilities regarding the prevention and detection of fraud.

The director has identified three key groups within the organisation.

Identify the group which is most associated with each of the following responsibilities.

	Board of Directors	**Audit Committee**	**All employees generally**
Ongoing monitoring and review of internal control and risk management systems.			
Maintaining sound systems of internal control.			
An implied duty to report suspected fraud to their superiors.			
An annual review of the effectiveness of internal controls and the reporting of this to shareholders.			

(0.5 marks each, total = 2 marks)

(Total: 4 marks)

LEADERSHIP AND MANAGEMENT

27 (a) FFC is a football club, based in country H, which is managed by four main individuals While FFC is a listed company, the majority of the shares are owned by a wealthy individual.

The Chair of the Board has significant authority within the club as he/she has been appointed directly by the majority shareholder, who listens to his/her advice on a regular basis. The Chair has no direct control over the pay and conditions of FFC employees, but the team typically follows his/her instructions due to his/her position.

FFC's coach is put in place to help the football team improve their skills. He/she is well respected in the football community and has significant experience of coaching football teams. The team follows his/her leadership as they believe he/she can significantly improve their chances of winning their matches.

The Chief Executive Officer (CEO) of FFC controls the pay and conditions of all the workers in FFC. He/she decides on bonuses and pay rises for the team and other workers.

The advisory coach is a retired footballer who has had a successful career in country H and is well known by the team. Most of the team players wish to copy his/her career and his/her skills.

Select which type of power each person below has displayed over the football team.

	Expert	Reward	Referent	Legitimate
FFC's Chair				
FFC's Coach				
FFC's CEO				
FFC's advisory coach				

(0.5 marks each, total = 2 marks)

(b) FFC has had some problems with employee behaviour in the last few seasons. In order to try and deal with this, FFC has held a seminar relating to leadership, management, authority and supervision.

The following sentences contain gaps which should contain one of the four terms.

FFC's CEO has shown a lack of _1_ as he/she has not ensured that FFC's resources have been well co-ordinated to maximise the strength of the team, while still having sufficient cash reserves to undertake all other necessary activities.

(i) Select the term that appropriately fills gap 1 above.

leadership/supervision/authority/management*

*delete as appropriate

FFC's coach has shown excellent _2_ skills. He/she has therefore been given responsibility for planning and controlling the actions of the team. He/she has improved the number of matches the team has won and has provided advice and support where necessary.

(ii) Select the term that appropriately fills gap 2 above.

leadership/supervision/authority/management*

*delete as appropriate **(1 mark each = 2 marks in total)**

(Total: 4 marks)

28 (a) According to Blake and Mouton's managerial grid, managers can be classified by their level of concern for people and concern for production.

		Concern for production	
		High	**Low**
Concern for people	**High**	A1	A2
	Low	A3	A4

In company X, the following managers have been ranked on the managerial grid.

Manager A has been classified as an 'impoverished manager'.

Manager B has been classified as a 'team manager'.

Manager C has been classified as a 'country club manager'.

Manager D has been classified as a 'task manager'.

(i) **For Manager A, highlight which combination of levels of concern apply from the grid above (i.e. A1).**

(ii) **For Manager B, highlight which combination of levels of concern apply from the grid above (i.e. A1).**

(iii) **For Manager C, highlight which combination of levels of concern apply from the grid above (i.e. A1).**

(iv) **For Manager D, highlight which combination of levels of concern apply from the grid above (i.e. A1).** **(0.5 marks each, total = 2 marks)**

(b) Here are four short descriptions of leadership and management theories:

A There is one best way to undertake every task

B Management can be split into five broad areas: planning, organising, commanding, co-ordinating and controlling

C Managers must control the needs of the task, individual and group.

D Managers can be either psychologically distant or psychologically close

Match EACH of the descriptions above with ONE of the following theories associated with it.

(i) **Adair's action-centred leadership**

(ii) **Fayol's functions of management**

(iii) **Fiedler's contingency theory**

(iv) **Taylor's theory of management** **(0.5 marks each, total = 2 marks)**

(Total: 4 marks)

29 (a) HB manufactures and sells pencils. Its main manager, Helena, has a key role which involves dividing the company's work into various individual tasks and assigning responsibility for these to different members of staff.

Which THREE of the following management functions does Helena exhibit by fulfilling this key role, as outlined by Fayol?

A Organisation

B Co-ordination

C Control

D Forecasting and planning

E Command

F Establish yardsticks **(0.5 marks each, total = 1.5 marks)**

(b) HB's manager has a number of key skills that are important to her role within the organisation:

A She collects and sorts out information on employee performance and the wider organisational context, helping the directors of the company make decisions.

B She continually looks for problems within the organisation and comes up with ideas for how to deal with them.

C She maintains contact with HB's suppliers and meets regularly to get information from them.

D She meets prospective new clients and tries to win their business by explaining what HB can do for them.

E She approves expenditure on fixed assets for the company.

Match EACH of the above descriptions to the appropriate management skill below, as per Mintzberg's management skills theory.

(i) Entrepreneur

(ii) Spokesperson

(iii) Liaison

(iv) Resource allocator

(v) Monitor **(0.5 marks each, total = 2.5 marks)**

(Total: 4 marks)

30 (a) PUG sells clothes and other accessories for pet dogs. It primarily sells through a small shop in an affluent area of the capital city of country P. It has been struggling to make a profit in recent years and its owner, Emma, is concerned about its long-term survival. PUG has a small but dedicated workforce, which is experienced in pet retail.

Emma is considering a number of possible approaches to managing her staff in this period of decline:

A She could ask the staff for ideas about how to turn the business around, though Emma would still have the final say on which, if any, of these ideas were used

B She could decide on a plan to improve the profitability of the business and simply inform her staff of how this will be implemented

C She could decide on a plan to improve profitability and explain the reasons and benefits of her proposals to her staff members

D She could come to a mutual decision with her staff about the best way forward for the company

Match EACH of the approaches above with ONE of the management styles below.

(i) Joins (democratic)

(ii) Consults (participative)

(iii) Tells (autocratic)

(iv) Sells (persuasive) **(0.5 marks each, total = 2 marks)**

(b) Emma has recently been reading an article on Adair's action-centred leadership model.

Which FOUR of the following statements are included in 'Task Needs' within Adair's action-centred leadership model?

A Communication

B Setting objectives

C Coaching

D Planning tasks

E Motivating

F Discipline

G Setting performance standards

H Allocating responsibilities **(0.5 marks each = 2 marks total)**

(Total: 4 marks)

31 (a) Jules has recently become a manager at YGH - a restaurant in a busy town. Jules is new to management having been a psychology student at a local university for a number of years. He is aware that YGH has had a number of problems with its staff behaviour in previous years and he wishes to understand the problems so that he can try to avoid similar issues reoccurring.

As such, Jules has undertaken some analysis work based on role theory and has identified the following issues:

A The waiters in the restaurant have different behaviour patterns to those of the kitchen staff, suggesting that both groups have their own defined norms of behaviour

B Waiters have a specific uniform that they must wear at all times to enable customers to identify them

C Waiters and bar staff often come into conflict as it is uncertain which group is responsible for taking drinks orders from customers

D Kitchen staff have previously reacted badly to being marked down on their appraisals for not reducing waste as they have argued that they are not responsible for this – despite management thinking that they should be

Match EACH of the above aspects of role theory with ONE of the following management terms.

(i) Role ambiguity

(ii) Role incompatibility

(iii) Role set

(iv) Role signs **(0.5 marks each, total = 2 marks)**

(b) Jules is considering building a small management team to help him run the restaurant. The team would be picked from existing employees – including waiters, bar staff and kitchen staff members – and would help Jules to make the decisions necessary to run YGH.

Which FOUR of the following statements are differences between YGH having a single manager or operating a management team?

A Improved mix of skills and abilities, which will help Jules given his relative inexperience

B Risk of increased social interaction between management team members, slowing decision-making down

C Reduced speed of decision making within YGH due to disagreements, conflicts and negotiations between team members

D As a team, YGH's staff may make less beneficial decisions as they are more likely to be compromises

E There will be reduced scope for flexibility if YGH has a team of managers

F As a team, each person in the management team will have increased personal responsibility for the decisions the team makes

G Operating as a management team means less group pressure to conform

H The creation of a team of managers is likely to reduce synergy within YGH

(0.5 marks each = 2 marks total)

(Total: 4 marks)

32 (a) CRU makes and sells garden furniture. The company is considering branching out into making household furniture and has set up a team to discuss how best to proceed with this new strategy.

The team is chaired by Ava – she is currently co-ordinating the different team members and ensuring that they meet regularly and stick to the agreed agenda. She has recently appointed Ella to the team. Ella has not proven to be a popular addition to the team as she tends to criticise any ideas thought up by other team members – though she has yet to produce any new ideas herself.

Charlotte is the main generator of ideas for the group. She has come up with designs for a wide range of possible products for CRU to make and sell. The other team member, Daniel, has been put in charge of ensuring that the team's goals are achieved on time and has chased other team members to ensure they complete agreed tasks on time.

According to Belbin's team roles theory, there are a number of roles that need to be fulfilled in any team.

Which FOUR of the following have been filled within CRU's project team?

A Shaper

B Plant

C Leader

D Monitor-evaluator

E Resource-investigator

F Team worker

G Company worker

H Finisher **(0.5 marks each = 2 marks total)**

(b) The managers of CRU are concerned that the team headed up by Ava is not working as effectively as possible. They are aware that, according to Tuckman's stages of group development model, the team should progress through a number of key stages, including:

A Norming

B Storming

C Dorming

D Performing

Match each of the above stages with ONE of the following statements (the most associated).

(i) The team decides on acceptable behaviour – including deciding what order each member presents their ideas in group meetings, as well as how other team members feedback their thoughts on these ideas

(ii) The team reaches its full potential and operates with maximum efficiency, with little conflict between the four members

(iii) The team has yet to decide on an acceptable format for criticism of ideas, meaning that meetings often descend into arguments

(iv) The team has generated a large number of ideas and the meetings typically turn into social gatherings where little is accomplished.

(0.5 marks each, total = 2 marks)

(Total: 4 marks)

33 (a) P operates a chain of hotels. The company directors are aware that the senior hotel managers may be difficult to replace, so they wish to ensure that hotel managers are adequately motivated.

Which FOUR of the above would be classified as helping to meet self-fulfilment or ego needs, according to Maslow's hierarchy of needs?

A Advancement opportunities

B Compatible, friendly work group

C Safe working conditions

D Pension

E Challenging work

F Permanent job contracts

G Merit pay rises (in spite of already attractive salaries)

H High status job titles

(0.5 marks each = 2 marks total)

(b) Below are a number of statements regarding motivation.

Which FOUR of the following statements are correct?

A Dealing with hygiene factors will cause positive employee motivation.

B Job enrichment often requires delegation by management.

C Job enlargement is often argued to have little motivational benefit.

D Job enlargement refers to giving staff higher level work than they currently undertake.

E Job rotation may be difficult in smaller organisations which have relatively few roles.

F Hygiene factors are issues that must be addressed to avoid job dissatisfaction.

G Job enrichment does not help an organisation with succession planning.

H Motivators are largely financial in nature.

(0.5 marks each, total = 2 marks)

(Total: 4 marks)

34 (a) According to Maslow's hierarchy of needs, different employees will be motivated by different things – either:

A Self-fulfilment

B Basic

C Social

D Safety

E Ego

Place the stages into the correct order, beginning with the lowest level of motivation.

(0.5 marks each, total = 2.5 marks)

(b) Below are a number of statements regarding motivation theories.

Which THREE of the following statements are correct?

A Maslow's theory may be summarised by saying that everyone wants certain things throughout life, and these can be placed in five ascending categories.

B Job enrichment involves moving employees to a new role periodically to keep them interested in their work.

C Theory Y employees are assumed to enjoy being directed and told what to do.

D A pleasant physical working environment would be classified as a 'hygiene factor' by Herzberg.

E Theory X employees are assumed to dislike work and responsibility.

F Management by objectives involves paying staff for each unit of product they produce.

(0.5 marks each, total = 1.5 marks)

(Total: 4 marks)

35 UHPD is a police force based in a town in country B. It is government funded and has a number of officers, who operate a wide range of roles – from patrols on foot around the town, highway and vehicle patrols, forensic analysis and administration.

Morale in the force has been low for several years, leading to a staffing crisis due to the high levels of staff turnover. Samuel is the head of the UHPD and has decided to investigate ways of motivating his workforce.

Samuel has investigated two major models to do with motivation – Herzberg's two-factor theory and McGregor's Theory X and Theory Y.

The following sentences contain gaps.

Samuel is considering the launch of a new policy that ensures that all members of staff are given an appropriate level of pay by formalising the grade boundaries of all staff. This will make pay fairer and will act as a _1_ for workers, hopefully reducing staff turnover.

(i) Select the term that appropriately fills gap 1 above.

hygiene factor/job enrichment/job rotation/motivator*

*delete as appropriate

Samuel has informed all managers within UHPD that they will be expected to delegate some responsibility down to more capable junior staff to improve UHPD's employee job design. Samuel referred to this in his report as _2_.

(ii) Select the term that appropriately fills gap 2 above.

hygiene factor/job enrichment/job rotation/motivator*

*delete as appropriate

Samuel has identified four managers within UHPD that have received high levels of complaints from their staff. They have adopted an authoritarian management style, assuming that employees are _3_. In fact, this is not the case and this mismatch in style has caused significant morale problems.

(iii) Select the term that appropriately fills gap 3 above.

Theory X/Theory Y*

*delete as appropriate

Samuel has decided against _4_ within UHPD as he is concerned that if staff are regularly moved between departments, their overall efficiency will drop.

(iv) Select the term that appropriately fills gap 4 above.

hygiene factor/job enrichment/job rotation/motivator*

*delete as appropriate **(1 mark each = 4 marks in total)**

(Total: 4 marks)

36 (a) JKJ is a large business that makes machinery. A new computer system is about to be introduced which will help boost the efficiency of the organisation by a significant percentage. The management of JKJ wishes to identify the various stages of the learning process and have therefore decided to use Kolb's model to help them plan the stages needed.

Kolb suggested that there were four main stages within the learning process:

A Concrete experience

B Abstract conceptualisation

C Active experimentation

D Reflective observation

Match EACH of the following training ideas to ONE of the stages of Kolb's learning process model (A, B, D or D).

(i) Allowing staff to input dummy data directly into the new system to help them understand how it works.

(ii) Getting staff to understand any mistakes they made when attempting to use the system in order to help them learn for future use.

(iii) Giving staff a manual to read about the new system.

(iv) Getting staff to apply what they know about the use of other, similar computer systems to the use of this new system. (0.5 marks each, total = 2 marks)

(b) The learning process contains three crucial concepts.

Identify which of the statements below relate to the terms training, education or development.

	Training	Education	Development
Defined as the activities which develop knowledge and skills for all aspects of life, rather than just a single job or task.			
Helping the individual to grow towards current and future roles within the organisation.			
Helps an individual carry out their work effectively.			
Tends to be job-oriented rather than personalised.			

(0.5 marks each, total = 2 marks)

(Total: 4 marks)

PERSONAL EFFECTIVENESS AND COMMUNICATION IN BUSINESS

37 (a) GGK is a small company which has grown rapidly in recent years. David, the main office manager, wishes to improve the company's quality of appraisals as he feels that this will help the company to effectively monitor the performance of its staff.

David has recently read an article which stated that the performance appraisal process usually followed four main stages:

A Action plan production

B Production of an appraisal report

C Identify the criteria for assessment

D Interview

Place the stages into the correct order, beginning with the lowest level of motivation.
(0.5 marks each, total = 2 marks)

(b) As part of the performance appraisal process, the company realises the importance of setting objectives that allow managers and employees to create, track and accomplish short and long term goals.

Which FOUR of the following are sound principles for devising performance measures?

A They should be easily achievable.

B They should be within the control of the individual.

C They should be observable or measurable.

D They should support the overall goals of the organisation.

E They should be subjective.

F The target date should always coincide with the end of the review year.

G They should be decided by the manager with no discussion between the manager and employees.

H They should be time-bound, with a realistic date for achievement.

(0.5 marks each, total = 2 marks)

(Total: 4 marks)

38 (a) Emir has recently started work at a factory and has been told that he has access to a coach and a mentor.

Identify which of the roles below relate to a coach or a mentor.

Role	**Coach**	**Mentor**
Giving general guidance and help to Emir.		
Improving Emir's skills on a particular machine.		
Acting as an impartial sounding board for any problems Emir might have.		
Has a defined time period in which it should be completed.		

(0.5 marks each, total = 2 marks)

(b) Emir has recently come into conflict with a number of other people since he started at the factory. His manager is aware that there are four main ways of dealing with conflict.

The following sentences contain gaps relating to the type of conflict management technique used.

Emir was in conflict with an existing employee, Oscar. The manager decided that the conflict was not significant enough to get involved and took no action, adopting a _1_ approach.

(i) Select the method of dealing with conflict that appropriately fills gap 1 above.

resolution/suppression/reduction/denial*

*delete as appropriate

Emir was also in conflict with another new employee, Leon. This was found to be because Leon was being paid more than Emir in spite of having equivalent experience and qualifications. The manager adopted a _2_ strategy and increased Emir's pay accordingly.

(ii) Select the method of dealing with conflict that appropriately fills gap 2 above.

resolution/suppression/reduction/denial*

*delete as appropriate **(1 mark each = 2 marks in total)**

(Total: 4 marks)

39 (a) Thomas works in a local government office. He has significant problems with time management and often feels that there are 'simply not enough hours in the day' for him to accomplish all of the tasks he has been given.

Thomas has compiled a list of issues that he feels may be preventing him from achieving good time management in his role.

Which FOUR of the following statements are most likely to be contributing to Thomas's poor time management?

A Thomas's job is dynamic and very unpredictable.

B Thomas is assertive and willing to tell his managers if he does not have time to complete a task.

C Many of the people that Thomas has to meet face-to-face are located far from his office.

D When in his office, Thomas operates a 'closed door' policy meaning that colleagues have to formally book time to discuss issues with him.

E The department that Thomas works for is bureaucratic, requiring significant amounts of paperwork to be undertaken for both major and minor tasks.

F Thomas's department makes extensive use of IT to aid communication between employees.

G Thomas dislikes keeping a diary and feels he never 'has any time' to complete one.

H Thomas is skilled at breaking larger jobs down into smaller tasks.

(0.5 marks each, total = 2 marks)

(b) Thomas's recent appraisal has led to the development of a personal development plan. This process falls into three main stages.

Identify the stage which is associated with each of the following activities.

Activity	**Analysis of Thomas's current position**	**Action plan**	**Goal setting**
Ensuring that all objectives set for Thomas are measurable.			
Carrying out a personal SWOT analysis for Thomas.			
Set specific targets for Thomas to work towards, along with details of how success will be measured.			
Identifying that Thomas has poor time management skills.			

(0.5 marks each, total = 2 marks)

(Total: 4 marks)

40 (a) **Which FOUR of the following statements are features of objectives?**

A Achievable

B Related

C Acceptable

D Timely

E Specific

F Measurable

G Quantitative

H Straightforward **(0.5 marks each, total = 2 marks)**

(b) Here are four short definitions of key types of communication:

A Communication between people at the same level within the organisation

B A lack of this means that managers get little feedback from their more junior employees

C This refers to communication between different levels and departments

D A lack of this means that junior employees will be unaware of their manager's plans and goals

Match EACH of the descriptions above with ONE of the following types of communication (A, B, C or D).

(i) Downwards communication

(ii) Upwards communication

(iii) Diagonal communication

(iv) Lateral communication **(0.5 marks each, total = 2 marks)**

(Total: 4 marks)

PROFESSIONAL ETHICS

41 (a) **Which FOUR of the following ethical terms are part of the IESBA code of ethics?**

A Honesty

B Objectivity

C Confidentiality

D Openness

E Trust

F Integrity

G Professional behaviour

H Transparency **(0.5 marks each, total = 2 marks)**

(b) Professional accountants can face a number of different ethical threats.

The following sentences contain gaps relating to a type of ethical threat faced.

An accountant previously suggested a new strategy to an organisation he/she prepares the accounts for. He/she has since been asked to examine the strategy to see if it has been a success. He/she therefore faces a major _1_ threat to his/her professional ethics.

(i) Select the ethical threat that appropriately fills gap 1 above.

self-interest/familiarity/advocacy/self-review*

*delete as appropriate

An accountant has been asked to work on the accounts for an organisation that is currently managed by his wife, exposing him to a threat of _2_.

(ii) Select the ethical threat that appropriately fills gap 2 above.

self-interest/familiarity/advocacy/self-review*

*delete as appropriate **(1 mark each = 2 marks in total)**

(Total: 4 marks)

42 (a) **Which FOUR of the following are safeguards that professional accountancy bodies are responsible for implementing?**

A Ethics training as part of professional training

B Regulatory monitoring and disciplinary procedures

C Creation of codes of conduct for each company

D Creating legally binding controls over accountant behaviour

E Developing internal complaints procedures for organisations

F Creation of corporate governance requirements

G Creating legally binding codes of conduct on corporate behaviour

H Creation of professional standards

(0.5 marks each, total = 2 marks)

(b) There are a number of differing approaches to ethics.

The following sentences contain gaps relating to the approach to ethics being used.

Company W has decided to press ahead with plans to open a new factory. It will have a detrimental effect on the environment and the local residents, but will make the company a significant profit. The company has therefore adopted a _1_ approach to ethics.

(i) Select the ethical approach that appropriately fills gap 1 above.

egoism/utilitarianism/pluralism/absolutism*

*delete as appropriate

If company W decided to redesign the factory in order to minimise the impact on the residents and environment, but still make an overall (though lesser) profit than before, its approach to ethics would now be _2_.

(ii) Select the ethical approach that appropriately fills gap 2 above.

egoism/utilitarianism/pluralism/absolutism*

*delete as appropriate **(1 mark each = 2 marks in total)**

(Total: 4 marks)

43 (a) Accountancy is an example of a profession.

Which FOUR of the following are features of a profession (as opposed to an occupation)?

A Legal backing for the status of 'profession'

B Limitation on the number of trainees that can be taken on each period

C Oversight by an international body

D Learning of specialist skills in a training period

E Compliance with an ethical code

F A certification process before being allowed to practise

G Rigorous selection of candidates before they are allowed to train

H Governance by a professional body

(0.5 marks each, total = 2 marks)

(b) Professional accountants have to abide by a number of ethical principles.

The following sentences contain gaps relating to one of the above ethical principles.

Zeinab is a qualified accountant. She has recently faced an ethical threat of self-review. If she does nothing to deal with this, she will have breached her requirement to act with _1_.

(i) Select the ethical principle that appropriately fills gap 1 above.

integrity/objectivity/confidentiality/professional competence*

*delete as appropriate

Eden has recently been undertaking an audit on KJH Co and has discovered that the company is paying its employees lower than the legal minimum wage. Reporting this information is not a breach of _2_ as there is a legal reason to do so.

(ii) Select the ethical principle that appropriately fills gap 2 above.

integrity/objectivity/confidentiality/professional competence*

*delete as appropriate

(1 mark each = 2 marks in total)

(Total: 4 marks)

Section 3

ANSWERS TO OBJECTIVE TEST QUESTIONS – SECTION A

THE BUSINESS ORGANISATION

1 D

Organisations do not have to create a product or service in order to be classified as an organisation. For example, an orchestra may be classed as an organisation, but it does not necessarily create a product.

2

Statement	**True**	**False**
Private companies can raise share capital by advertising to the general public.		✓
Private companies can raise share capital from venture capitalists	✓	

Only public companies can advertise their shares to the general public. Both private and public companies can raise share capital from venture capitalists.

3 C

The primary role of the public sector is to provide essential government services that are necessary for the functioning of a society, such as education, healthcare and infrastructure. Option A is typically a characteristic of the private sector. Option B is indicative of non-profit organisations or charities, rather than the public sector and option D describes the operations of a cooperative, which is distinct from the public sector as the public sector serves the broader public and is funded through taxes, not subscriptions.

4 C

This is the definition of the term 'synergy'. Note that organisations may also allow specialisation, meaning that individuals can focus on becoming highly skilled in just one area.

5 A

As public limited companies are able to sell their shares to the public, they will often find it easier to raise large amounts of capital for growth, if needed. This may be much harder for partnerships and sole traders. Only public companies can sell shares to the public, companies may be owned by only one shareholder and shareholders enjoy limited liability.

6 B

Partnerships and companies would both usually be profit seeking. While government departments are likely to be not-for-profit, they would be part of the public sector. Therefore only charities would be likely to be both private AND not-for-profit.

7 C

Co-operatives are organised solely to meet the needs of the member-owners. Non-governmental organisations (NGOs) do not have profit as a primary goal and are not linked to national governments. Charities may be examples of NGOs. Private limited companies have shareholders, not members.

8 B

Westeros is a profit-seeking organisation – given that its fifteen owners own 'shares', it must be a private limited company. As such, only B is likely to be appropriate from the options provided. Central government funding is usually for public sector organisations, donations would usually be the major source of funding for charities and Westeros cannot issues shares to the public as it is a private limited company.

9

Statement	**True**	**False**
Not-for-profit organisations (NFPs) have varied objectives, which depend on the needs of their members or the sections of society they were created to benefit.	✓	
The primary objective of government-funded organisations is to reduce costs of their operations and thus minimise the burden on tax payers.		✓

NFPs may have radically different objectives – a charity may aim to help, say, animals under threat of extinction while a hospital may wish to treat its patients as effectively as possible.

Government funded organisations are usually concerned with providing basic government services. This does not always involve minimising the costs of their operations.

10 B

In a limited company, the owners (shareholders) are separate from the managers (board of directors).

BUSINESS ORGANISATION AND STRUCTURE

11 B

Because the entrepreneurial structure is run by one person who makes all the decisions, this powerful individual will have strong control over the organisation and its strategic direction, leading to better goal congruence.

12 B

An organisational chart is primarily used to depict the hierarchy and reporting relationships within an organisation, clarifying roles and responsibilities. Outlining the organisation's financial performance is typically done through financial statements. Providing a detailed list of employees and their qualifications is more relevant to human resources documentation, not an organisational chart. Tracking sales and marketing strategies would be done through strategic plans or marketing documents.

13 A

If H wants to manage each product separately, it will need to adopt either a matrix or divisional approach, as these would allow the creation of separate divisions for each product. However, H wishes to keep its administrative costs as low as possible. As the matrix structure has high admin costs due to high numbers of managers, A should adopt a divisional approach.

14 D

The granting of authority over each geographic area to geographic bosses results in a potential loss of control over key operating decisions. This weakness is also present in the Product/Division/Department structure.

15

Statement	True	False
Tall organisations typically have narrow spans of control.	✓	
A 'flat' organisation is one that has a short scalar chain.	✓	

16 D

Centralisation involves most decisions being made centrally within the organisation (i.e. at head office level). This means less training for more junior/local staff as well as better goal congruence as all decisions within the organisation are made by the same, senior group of managers. Options (ii) and (iii) are advantages of decentralisation.

17 A

Virtual organisations exist as a network of contracts with third party suppliers and will outsource all major functions. Hollow organisations only outsource non-core functions.

18 D

The description best matches a modular structure, where some parts of a product are manufactured by external companies rather than by the manufacturer itself.

19 B – FALSE

Offshoring typically involves the transfer of a function to an overseas location to reduce running costs. It would not normally involve transferring existing staff members to the other country.

20 B – FALSE

'Shared services' typically involves streamlining operations in order to reduce costs. It will also involve improving consistency over the way the service is undertaken and often leads to the service charging the other parts of the business to use its resources (i.e. it is run like a business).

21 B

Strategic planning involves making plans for the whole business, such as which locations to open, which markets to enter or exit and whether to raise cash from investors. As such, Stark's decision would fall into this category.

22 A

Operational planning involves practical, day-to-day strategies. As such, junior management would be best placed to undertake this level of planning.

23 C

This would normally be the function of the marketing department.

24 A

'Place' involves where the business sells its goods. For a high-street retailer this would be their stores. For an online retailer, it is more likely to be their website.

25 B

This is a philosophy of business that permeates all areas, focusing attention on the customer.

A = a sales orientation.

26 B

The basic mix tends to be used by organisations selling a tangible product (as opposed to a service).

27 D

While the 4Ps are product, place, promotion and price, don't forget that there are other elements that have subsequently been added to the marketing mix. These are people, processes and physical evidence.

28

Situation	Product	Place
Arryn Co manufactures and sells board games. It is currently considering the packaging, quality and design of the board games as part of a strategic review.	✓	
A key decision when reviewing the marketing mix is whether to sell directly to the consumer or indirectly through an intermediary.		✓

29 D

This would be a classic example of price discrimination – selling the same product at different prices to different markets/sections of the market.

30 C

The first product is cheap to attract customers but the second is expensive.

31 D

Segmentation would occur at the strategic choice stage as this enables the organisation to target attractive sections of the market.

32 A

Promotion follows the mnemonic 'AIDA' – awareness, interest, desire, action.

ORGANISATIONAL CULTURE IN BUSINESS

33

Statement	True	False
Culture was expressed by Handy as 'the sum of the belief, knowledge, attitudes, norms and customs that prevail in an organisation'.		✓
The tales of company creation, such as difficulties the founder had to face and how they managed to overcome them successfully often form a part of organisational culture.	✓	

Handy expressed culture as 'the way we do things around here', so statement 1 is false. However, history of the organisation plays an important role in shaping the mindset of the employees as it creates examples for them to follow in the future. This makes statement 2 correct.

34 A

Dress codes are usually seen as part of artefacts. This is because they are easy to observe.

35 B

This was a key finding of Schein's analysis.

36 B

Schein described these aspects of culture as basic assumptions and values. The other two levels are espoused values (strategies and goals, including slogans) and artefacts, which are the aspects of culture that are easy to see.

37 D

The cultural types identified by Handy are role culture, person culture, task culture and power culture.

38 A

It can either lead to improved motivation or increased inefficiency depending on its nature. This is one of the reasons managers need to be aware of the informal organisation that exists within their business.

39 A

A person culture focuses on recognising and valuing the contributions of each individual, where they work together to meet the overall goals of the organisation often to satisfy the requirements of a prominent individual e.g. barrister, chef.

40 C

Power cultures occur when there is one major source of power – often found in small owner managed businesses where the owner has total control over the business.

41 A

By definition. High motivation towards achievement and success represents values of competitiveness, ambition and accumulation of wealth, rather than being motivated more by work life balance, quality of life and relationships at work.

42 B

Bureaucratic businesses are evidence of high uncertainty avoidance as they give staff defined rules to work with. The fact that junior staff have a say in the running of the business is evidence of low power distance.

43 'The **informal organisation** is the network of relationships that exist within an organisation and arises through common interests and friendships between members of staff.'

The informal organisation evolves over time and is a network of relationships within an organisation that arise due to common interests or friendships. The informal organisation can either enhance or hold back the business since it often embraces both advantages (e.g. higher levels of motivation) and disadvantages (e.g. opposition to change).

44 C

If managers work along with the informal groups within the organisation, it should improve motivation and productivity of workers. The informal organisation often encourages individuals to conform to the organisation's norms (which can cause increased resistance to change), but does tend to allow strong interdivisional communication.

INFORMATION TECHNOLOGY AND INFORMATION SYSTEMS IN BUSINESS

45

Statement	**True**	**False**
Big data contains both financial and non-financial data.	✓	
Cloud computing allows storage and accessing of data programs over the internet instead of on the computer's hard drive.	✓	

Both statements are correct. Big data refers to large volume of data, many sources of data and many types of data. Cloud computing is the practice of using a network of remote servers hosted on the Internet to store, manage, and process data, rather than a local server or a personal computer.

46

Statement	**True**	**False**
A spreadsheet can perform the task of presenting numerical data in the form of graphs and charts.	✓	
A spreadsheet can perform the task of applying 'What if?' scenarios.	✓	

47 D

The information has not been put in a user-friendly manner and cannot be easily understood by the users.

48 C

This is a valid concern, especially for small businesses or specific applications where the initial and ongoing costs of database setup, management and maintenance might not be justifiable compared to the benefits gained.

49 C

An EIS is distinguished from a DSS by supporting decision-making at a higher and less structured level.

50

Statement	**True**	**False**
Blockchain technology presents the possibility of an accounting ledger that can be continuously updated and verified without the threat of being altered or corrupted.	✓	
Phishing is a type of computer virus.		✓

Only the first statement is correct. Phishing an attempt by criminals to try to obtain sensitive information by presenting themselves as a trusty source.

51

	Decision support system	Expert system	Management information system
This system type converts data from a transaction processing system into information for monitoring performance and maintaining co-ordination.			✓
When the government authority at the end of the tax year sends thousands of notifications to people with an estimate of the tax they need to pay, these letters are likely to be produced by this system type.		✓	

52 D

The link between the inventory store and the component suppliers expands FFK's network and so exposes them to a cyber-security threat. Phone orders are a potential business risk but not a cyber-security threat.

53 C

The security of data is a major concern in the majority of organisations and if the organisation lacks the resources to manage data then there is likely to be a greater risk of leaks and losses.

54 C and D

Automation and artificial intelligence support automatic and intelligent processing of transactional information to free the accountant to work on value-adding services rather than focussing on low-level transactions. Distributed ledger technology reduces (not increases) the need for auditors to audit all transactions.

STAKEHOLDERS

55 A

Internal includes employees and managers/directors; connected includes shareholders, customers, suppliers, and finance providers. The third stakeholder group is external which includes the community at large, government and trade unions.

56 C

Pressure groups are external to the organisation, but can sometimes influence a company's decisions. They have no contractual link to the organisation, however, meaning that they are also secondary.

57 C

In this case, A's shareholders have a high level of power, but a low level of interest.

58 B

This approach is referred to as Keep Informed, whereas minimal effort implies that stakeholders will accept what they are told.

59 A

This is correct as customers have an interest in higher levels of product and service quality and, in the short term at least, satisfying this interest is likely to reduce the profits and dividends available to shareholders.

60 A

If stakeholders have little interest in the business and no real power, there is no point to a business doing more than minimal effort.

EXTERNAL ANALYSIS – POLITICAL AND LEGAL FACTORS

61 C

A = Technological heading, B = Economic heading, D = Social heading.

62 A

Privatisation refers to a government selling its assets.

63 A

Other sources include the International Court of Justice, European parliament, European courts and certain international agreements, e.g. World Trade Organisation rules.

64 C

The Act imposes obligations on the Data Controller (an individual or an organisation who has information about the individual), and the rights of the Data Subject (individual about whom the information is held).

65

	Yes	**No**
Right of subject access – individuals are entitled to be told whether the data controller holds personal data about them.	✓	
Right to prevent processing for the purposes of direct marketing.	✓	

66 D

The credit file company must provide Alex with access to his credit file. However, Alex does not have the right to request this for free and may have to pay a fee.

Alex can also use typical data protection legislation to block direct marketing. However, junk mail is likely to be sent to a large number of recipients and therefore is not direct marketing.

EXTERNAL ANALYSIS – ECONOMIC FACTORS

67 C

The equilibrium point of demand and supply curves is where the quantity demanded by consumers exactly matches the quantity supplied by producers. Producers are motivated by profit. When the selling price of a good increases, the potential profit for producing and selling that good also increases. Therefore, a higher price encourages existing suppliers to increase their production and may also attract new producers to the market, leading to a rise in the total quantity supplied. This is represented by an upward sloping supply curve.

68 B

In the short term, as production increases, the average cost per unit will *fall* because fixed costs (such as factory rent) are spread over a larger number of units.

69 A

By definition. A price change will cause movement up or down the demand curve. A change in the conditions of demand (i.e. tastes or population) will shift the entire curve either left or right.

70 C

The fact that the units sold fall by more than the price increase indicates that this product is relatively elastic. This would give a PED of more than 1.

71 A

Expansion and contraction in demand will occur when the price charged by H for the GHF300 changes. A reduction in the selling price is likely to mean that more people want to buy the vehicle and demand will expand.

The other three options will all create a shift in the demand curve, where more units of the product will be sold, even if the company maintains its current prices.

72 B

The opposite is true – perfect markets assume that all goods sold by suppliers are homogenous (identical).

73 A

A market with only a few dominant organisations is referred to as an oligopoly.

74 C

This type of market occurs when a business has many different competitors, but eac h offersa somewhat differentiated product.

75 D

The other factors are the availability of substitutes and the definition of the market.

76 A and D

Upwards shifts in the supply curve are caused by increases in the costs of making and/or selling the product. This means that, even if the selling price stays constant, the profitability of the product will fall, meaning that suppliers like L will not wish to produce as many units of the product as they are less profitable.

Options A and D both involve the costs of production rising. These would therefore cause an upward shift in the curve. Options B and C are the opposite, leading to a decline in the costs of production of the windows and therefore a downward shift in the curve.

77 C

Low price elasticity of demand indicates that even a significant change in the selling price will have little effect on the number of units that customers demand. If the customers spend a high proportion of their income on E's product, any rise in the selling price could make it unaffordable, leading to a significant fall in demand. This would therefore indicate HIGH elasticity of demand. If the product is not seen as a necessity, it would again mean that if the price rises, customers may no longer feel that they have to keep buying the product, again leading to a significant decline in demand. A high number of substitutes would enable customers to easily switch to cheaper rival products if E raises its prices. If, however, customers buy the product habitually (or automatically) without ever really checking the price (as often happens with gum, or newspapers), a significant rise in prices will have little impact on sales volume.

78 A

The government is setting a minimum price for labour. This will increase the supply of labour, as work becomes more attractive to the population of country X – but will reduce the demand for labour from companies as it becomes more expensive. This is likely to lead to a surplus of labour, leading to rising unemployment. The rising cost of wages is likely to lead manufacturing companies to avoid making items that are labour intensive and move towards automation where possible.

79 D

As production increases, the cost per unit will initially fall due to the larger number of units being made which the total cost is spread over. However, even within the short-term, as the number of units of output grows, efficiency of the production system will fall, leading to a rise in average cost per unit again. This is known as the law of diminishing returns. Diseconomies of scale occur over the long-term.

80 B

This is sometimes referred to as demand-deficient, persistent or Keynesian unemployment. Keynesian economists refer to this as a deflationary gap and would seek to remove it by boosting demand. Monetarists would seek to reduce cyclical unemployment by appropriate supply-side measures as they would argue that cyclical unemployment does not really exist.

81 A

Rapid growth tends to lead to rising incomes, which often increases demand by the population for imported goods.

82 B

Given the high rate of unemployment, the government of country Y is likely to be suffering from a fall in its tax receipts (unemployed individuals have lower earnings to tax). The government will also have to pay more in social security to support the increasing number of workers who are without jobs. The other three statements are correct.

83

	Yes	No
Economic growth	✓	
Money supply management		✓

Macroeconomic policy objectives tend to be management of economic growth, inflation, employment and a sustainable balance of payments. While the money supply may be used by the government to achieve its policies, it is not an objective in itself.

84 D

Expectations are often self-fulfilling as people adjust their behaviour based on the predictions made, such as the belief that house prices will continue to grow will cause people to buy a house to make a quick gain, which in its turn inflates the prices of houses.

85 B

A deflationary gap occurs when there is insufficient demand in the economy. Having a budget deficit means that the government is putting money in the economy, for example by employing more people, who will use their earning to buy goods produced in the country, thus giving jobs to even more people. C and D are a part of the monetary policy.

86 D

A recession starts when demand begins to fall and leads to reduced purchases of raw materials and increased unemployment; this in turn leads to reduced household incomes and a further fall in demand, which can result in a slump.

87 A

Increasing interest rates encourages saving, discourages consumer expenditure and discourages borrowing/ investment. Increasing taxation lowers demand in the economy because people have less money after tax for consumption or saving/investment. Increasing public expenditure should increase the level of consumer demand.

88 B

The country is exporting too much, which means that factors of production could be fully utilised, therefore the costs of an additional unit of output will be higher than the costs of previous units, thus prices will be raised causing inflation.

89 D

'Demerit' goods are such things as illegal drugs. A, B and C are examples of the positive aspects of growth. A = real growth. B = the benefits of growth are being evenly distributed. C = the population, on average, is better off.

90 A

Keynes argued that it was the government's role to move the economy to a better equilibrium, i.e. one closer to full employment. This involved the government borrowing money and injecting it into the economy to stimulate economic growth – or slowing down the economy by increasing levels of taxation.

91 A

The classical approach emphasises the concept of free markets leading to efficient allocation of resources with minimal government intervention. The focus on limiting government intervention and reducing fiscal deficits reflects the classical belief in self-regulating markets and the importance of maintaining balanced budgets over active government spending to manage the economy. Monetarist economics primarily focuses on controlling the money supply to manage inflation and stabilise the economy. While it also supports free markets, its core emphasis is more on monetary policy than on fiscal deficits and government intervention. Keynesian (demand-side economics advocates for active government intervention, particularly through fiscal policy and increasing public expenditure.

92 A

Aggregate demand is calculated as consumer spending + investment by firms + government spending + exports – imports. If all else stays constant, a rising trade deficit means that imports are rising faster than exports, lowering the aggregate demand.

If the imports are also increasing in price, this will cause inflation within country C – specifically imported inflation. Monetary inflation occurs when the money supply expands too rapidly.

93 C

Expenditure reducing strategies involve the government shrinking the domestic economy to reduce the demand for imports. A budget surplus would accomplish this.

Expenditure-switching strategies encourage consumers to switch to domestically produced goods. The other three options are examples of these.

94 A

Remember that Keynes' approach is also referred to as 'demand-side' economics as it involves the government stepping in to manipulate the level of demand in the economy as needed.

EXTERNAL ANALYSIS – SOCIAL, ENVIRONMENTAL AND TECHNOLOGICAL FACTORS

95 D

Population growth can be important to a range of organisations in the private sector – high growth, for instance, may indicate growth in the market for the organisation's products or services.

The definition given for 'attitudes' is actually the definition of 'tastes'. Attitudes represent a person or group's like or dislike for a thing.

96 B

An aging population will not automatically mean that high-tech products will fall in popularity – though the businesses that manufacture and sell them may need to adjust their products and marketing to target older users. The second statement is correct.

97 C

Outsourcing means that some of the processes previously undertaken by the company itself are now being transferred to an external supplier.

98 D

Carbon footprint refers to the volume of carbon emissions produced by the company. The goal of social responsibility is to be conscious of the impact operations have on the environment and the planet. It is possible for the firm's products to be boycotted if customers believe that it acts in a socially irresponsible way.

99 C

Delayering refers to the reduction in the number of levels of management, making organisational structure flatter. Managers can use technology to help keep in touch with staff, thus freeing more time for more urgent tasks.

100 A

Merely rebranding a product is unlikely to reduce a company's impact on its environment. The other three, however, should all help.

101 B

This is the official definition of sustainability.

102 C

Outsourcing is likely to increase the risk of security breaches as a third party will have access to Lannister's systems. Outsourcing IT would be likely to mean the closure of Lannister's own IT department, which will mean the loss of skilled staff. This will make it difficult for Lannister to bring IT back in-house in the future. In addition, such a move would be likely to cause a loss of competitive advantage as Lannister will have no way to create its own, unique systems.

103 A

By not creating waste, an organisation is ensuring that resources are more likely to be available to future generations, improving sustainability.

COMPETITIVE FACTORS

104 C

Threat of substitutes refers to people's tendency to replace one product with another.

105 D

The assessment will be in three steps, analysing how the firm can achieve a competitive advantage, the main competitive forces in the industry and how parts of the firm contribute to its competitiveness.

106 C

Low customer switching costs make it easier for a new entrant to attract customers away from existing firms, thereby increasing the threat of new entrants.

107 D

Outbound logistics includes packaging and delivery.

108 B

The receipt of the cable from the manufacturers would be inbound logistics. Cutting it down into lengths forms the operations of AAH. Procurement would be sourcing suppliers for the cable, while infrastructure would include the structure of the organisation (i.e. centralised purchasing of cable).

109 B

Differentiation involves making your product stand out from rivals with additional features or a stronger brand. This would usually allow you to charge a premium for your product.

110 A

H is targeting a niche part of the market and providing goods and services to match its needs.

111 B

The approach involves breaking the firm down into five 'primary' and four 'support' activities and then looking at each to see if they give a cost advantage or quality advantage.

112 B

The term 'administration' indicates that Steve's role is a support activity, as this term is used in the model. The description of his role could only reinforce this conclusion. Likewise, 'information technology' indicates that Sam performs a support role. Finally, although Porter's term 'procurement' is not included in the statement, Sunny's responsibilities for dealing with suppliers of inventory and capital equipment are sufficient to conclude that Sunny also occupies a support role.

Note: Instead of applying this process of elimination, candidates could have considered the essential differences between primary and support activities, which would have led them to the correct conclusion.

113 A

It is likely to be a strength. It's clearly not a weakness or threat and given that is an internal issue, it should not be classed as an opportunity – although it may enable AZ to pursue any opportunities it identifies.

114 A

By definition.

PROFESSIONAL ETHICS IN ACCOUNTING AND BUSINESS

115 D

Amelia is arguing that she needed to use the money for an ethical reason, so the theft was justifiable. This would be an example of a relativist approach, where actions are justified based on their circumstances. The action is not being argued to be for the 'greater good' or for all stakeholders (presumably the theft will not be good for the shareholders of LGH!) so Amelia is not a utilitarian or a pluralist.

116 A

By definition. Professions also require the mastering of specialist skills, governance by a professional organisation and a process of certification of new members.

117 B

The remaining two ethical principles are integrity and objectivity.

118

Statement	**True**	**False**
All ACCA members must comply with the Fundamental Principles, whether or not they are in practice.	✓	
Professionals owe an obligation to society as well as a duty to their client.	✓	

Those failing to observe the standards expected of them may be called before the ACCA's Disciplinary Committee and required to explain their conduct.

The IFAC code (which is the basis of the ACCA code) states in its introduction that 'a professional accountant's responsibility is not exclusively to satisfy the needs of an individual client or employer.'

The professional accountant, therefore, has a duty to act in the public interest as well as in the interests of their employer and the shareholders.

119 B

The definition given is that of integrity.

120 A

Egoists will choose the option that most benefits themselves, which would appear to be accepting the bribe. Utilitarians would accept the bribe if it caused a favourable outcome for the greatest number of people – not necessarily all stakeholders (this is pluralism).

121 D

Professions must have: a process of certification, a period of training leading to the mastering of specialised skills, an ethical code and governance by a professional organisation. Occupations do not need any of these. Both organisations and professions would be expected to comply with legislation.

122 C

An accountant should first raise the issue with whoever is in charge of ethics or governance within the organisation (i.e. the Compliance Officer). If this does not solve the issue, the accountant can take legal/professional advice from their professional body. Finally, if the issue is still unresolved, the matter may be reported to the relevant authorities.

123 B

Noor recommended the purchase of the business and is now having to review the quality of that decision. This makes it difficult for her to be objective and criticise the prospects of the business.

124 B

They are all ACCA safeguards, except for B, which is a safeguard that an individual company may put in place in order to minimise the risk of unethical behaviour.

125 B

Lorenzo is a utilitarian – looking to benefit the greatest number of people. Note that 'individualist' is not an approach to ethical decision-making.

126 A

The acronym 'HOTTER' can be used to remember these – honesty, openness, transparency, trust, empowerment and respect.

127 C

This is the definition of respect. Empowerment is getting employees involved in making their own decisions.

128 A

Deontological ethics is linked to the concept of absolutism – things are inherently wrong or right, regardless of the consequences.

GOVERNANCE AND SOCIAL RESPONSIBILITY IN BUSINESS

129 D

Reasons for the separation of ownership and management include the suggestion that specialist management can run the business better than those who own the business.

130 D

Directors, who are placed in control of resources that they do not own and are effectively agents of the shareholders, should be working in the best interests of the shareholders. However, they may be tempted to act in their own interests, for example by voting themselves huge salaries. The background to the agency problem is the separation of ownership and control – in many large companies the people who own the company (the shareholders) are not the same people as those who control the company (the board of directors).

131 B

As this will serve as a financial motivator and will align directors' interests with those of the shareholders.

132 B

The stakeholders are all those influenced by, or those who can influence the company's decisions and actions.

133 B

Sustainable development focuses on the future, making sure that our actions today do not jeopardise the future of the planet.

134 A

Many customers are choosing to buy Fairtrade products and shareholders are investing in environmentally-friendly companies as people are becoming more aware of the impact their actions have on the environment and society as a whole.

135 B – False

Shareholders can become directors. The agency problem refers to the problem of directors acting in their own personal best interests rather than those of the company and its owners.

136 D

Owning the shares creates a direct link between a company's performance and the NED's wealth, thus rendering them non-independent. Note that NEDs should not have worked for the company as an employee for the last five years or serve as a NED for more than 9 years with the same company. It is worth noting that non-independent NEDs can be chosen by the company – as long as there is a majority of independent NEDs on the board and appropriate disclosures are made.

137 A

An audit committee should be comprised of at least three members, all of whom should be independent non-executive directors.

138 B

Companies are required by law to send a copy (or a summarised version) to each shareholder. Most companies will post a copy on their web site or will provide a paper- based copy free of charge to any member of the public who requests one.

139 C

Distractors A and B should have been eliminated by the references to 'legally binding', 'must adhere' and 'detailed rules'. Distractor D suggests that corporate governance relates to management and administration at the operational level, where in fact corporate governance is about ensuring standards are set at the highest levels of an organisation through appropriate mechanisms, which can filter down to operations.

Codes of practice are usually associated with a principles-based approach rather than a rules-based approach, so successful candidates were directed to the correct response by the words 'guidance' and 'should adopt'.

140 A

Ad-hoc stands for 'for the purpose' and the committee is likely to be disbanded as soon as the issue for which it was created is resolved.

141 D

Part of the Chair's role is to maintain order, whereas A, B and C are a part of the role of Secretary.

142 B

Other duties of the committee secretary include preparing the location; assisting the chair; acting on and communicating decisions.

143 D

The remuneration committee is usually focused on Director's remuneration package. It does not examine the pay and grading for all employees.

144 B

Committees tend to be slower at decision making than individuals as there is more conflict/disagreement between individual members.

145 A

Decisions are often compromises, meaning that decisive action may not be taken.

LAW AND REGULATION GOVERNING ACCOUNTING

146 D

Companies house deals with incorporation and dissolution on companies, as it examines and stores companies' information as per Companies Act requirements.

147 B

National legislation places a requirement on companies in respect of mandatory reports to government and shareholders (and usually both). This is to ensure that limited companies adhere to certain minimum standards. In many countries an underlying purpose of this is to protect prospective and existing investors in the company, and to minimise the possibility of tax evasion.

Codes of corporate governance are now used extensively in countries that adopt a principles-based approach to corporate governance. Such codes are not underpinned by legislation and are voluntary in nature. Companies and other organisations are expected to comply with the provisions of the codes, or to explain to shareholders why they are not doing so.

International Accounting Standards seek to achieve consistency in reporting across international frontiers. They affect the content and presentation of the company accounts, but it is up to governments and their agents to decide on the requirements for preparation and filing of accounts.

148 D

Company financial statements must be free from material misstatement. They may still contain immaterial or insignificant mistakes or errors and be considered true and fair.

149

	Yes	**No**
Suspension of FVF's shares by the stock exchange.	✓	
Tax authority investigation into FVF.	✓	

150 C

The IASB's aims are to develop a single set of high quality, understandable and enforceable global accounting standards and to co-operate with national accounting standard-setters to achieve convergence in accounting standards around the world.

151 B

Options A and D are the responsibility of the IFRS Advisory Council (AC), while option C is the role of the IASB.

152 B

FRSs in the UK are written by the ASB (Accounting Standards Board). They largely replaced SSAPs, although any SSAPs which have not yet been replaced by an FRS will still be in force.

ACCOUNTING AND FINANCE FUNCTIONS WITHIN BUSINESS

153 C

The treasurer would also be responsible for debt strategy, currency management, banking forecasting and risk management.

154 A

Management accounting would focus on internal stakeholders.

155 A

While it is recommended, it is ultimately up to the organisation itself.

156 A

Small companies do not have to be audited. As the company is owner-managed the agency problem will not be relevant.

157 B

The financial accounting department would be responsible for recording financial transactions and reporting to shareholders. The management accountants would be responsible for putting together standard cost cards.

158 B

Financial accountants would usually prepare the external financial statements, including the statement of cash flows, the income statement and the statement of financial position. A and C would normally be the responsibility of management accountants, while D would usually be undertaken by the treasury function.

159

Angelo decided to record the purchases made on the 2nd of April 200X in tax year ending 31st of March 200X. The authorities will likely classify this as tax evasion.

This is tax evasion as the company is illegally reducing its tax liability. Note that it cannot be both evasion AND avoidance simultaneously.

160 D

Tax avoidance is used to describe schemes which, whilst they are legal, are designed to defeat the intentions of the law makers. Thus, once a tax avoidance scheme becomes public knowledge, the law makers will usually step in to change the law to stop the scheme from working.

161 C

A, B and D are not true. They describe advantages of using the issue of share capital to finance investment.

162 B

A is incorrect as VDF will never have to pay dividends if it cannot afford them. Equity finance is not secured on the company's assets, so C is incorrect. D is also incorrect as dividends are not tax allowable, meaning that the issue of shares is unlikely to directly affect VDF's tax liability.

163 A

Working capital is the capital available for conducting the day-to-day operations of an organisation.

164 B

Budgets lay out the planned income and expenditure for the coming period. Variance reports compare actual results to the budget for a period. The statement of financial position is the responsibility of financial accountants.

165 C

Integrated reports will provide users with additional information on anything the organisation feels they would be interested in, such as the company's environmental impact or sustainability in the period.

166 D

Costing of units would the purpose of a cost schedule or standard cost card.

167 B

The six capitals are financial, manufactured, intellectual, human, social and relationship, and natural capital.

168

	SOPL	**SOFP**
The net assets of HGF		✓
HGF's gross profit for the year	✓	

Remember that the SOFP shows the assets, liabilities and capital of the company, while the SOPL shows the income and expenses (and therefore the profit or loss) of the business in the period.

FINANCIAL SYSTEMS AND PROCEDURES

169 A

Reconciliation of supplier statements would identify any discrepancies between the amounts that Victoria's business believes it owes suppliers and the amount its suppliers believe it owes them. This should identify any incorrect payments that have been made. Matching the payment amount to the original invoice and ensuring that the payment is correctly authorised could also help.

170 A

By matching the GDN to the original order, JBB will be ensuring that it is sending the correct items to each customer.

171 C

The fourth purpose is prevention of fraud. Control systems may indirectly improve profitability through increased efficiency, etc, but it is not one of their primary purposes.

172 D

Customer identity and ability to pay should be verified prior to a sale being processed. A, B, and C are good control measures, but are not directly relevant to prompt payment.

173 B

BACS is an automated bank transfer when the money is sent directly to an employee's bank account, which makes the transaction easy to trace and more secure.

174 A

As it is company policy to record goods only if accepted then a comparison on invoices with goods received records would identify if the goods had not been accepted. This would then prevent the invoice from being processed.

175 A

The usual procedure is for the individual responsible for the petty cash to present the receipts and vouchers in order to obtain replenishment.

However, two people should open the post and list the contents.

176 D

The purposes of organisational control are to safeguard company assets, ensure efficiency and prevent fraud and errors.

THE RELATIONSHIP BETWEEN ACCOUNTING AND OTHER BUSINESS FUNCTIONS

177 D

The accounting department can help ensure a profitable selling price is used for E's products.

178 A

Option A would most likely be a marketing or service provision crossover with the accounting department.

179

'Services have certain qualities which distinguish them from products. Due to their intangibility, physical elements such as tickets, confirmations and certificates are important part of the service provision.'

Intangibility refers to the fact that there are no material or physical aspects to a service. Physical elements help to reduce this effect and make the provision more concrete for the customer.

180 D

Inseparability looks at the fact that services cannot easily be distinguished from the person providing the service. If the taxi driver behaves badly, the customer will perceive the service itself as being poor.

AUDIT AND FINANCIAL CONTROL

181 B

The internal audit also makes recommendations for the achievement of company objectives.

C is the role of the external auditors.

182 A

Statement 2 is part of the definition of internal control – while there is crossover between the two topics, make sure you know the differences between them!

183 B

They are employed by the management of the company and yet are expected to give an objective opinion on matters for which management are responsible.

184 D

The audit committee would act as an interface between the directors and internal auditors to reduce the problem of independence.

185 A and D

Statement B is the wrong way round – external auditors test the underlying transactions that make up the financial statements, while internal auditors test the operations of the company's systems. Statement C is also incorrect as internal audit is not usually a legal requirement, though corporate governance principles state that if an internal audit function is not present, the company should annually assess the need for one.

186 A

Guidance for an internal audit is limited to fundamental principles and a small quantity of standards and these factors are largely responsible for the greater flexibility in how the work is done. However, there is no legal requirement for an internal auditor to possess an accounting qualification, though it is highly desirable.

187 A

Control environment refers to the overall attitude of managers to the importance of internal controls.

188 D

A TPS records and summarises the basic transactions of the organisation. This would be summarised and form part of the financial statements of the organisation. As such, it would form part of the retail company's information systems.

189 B

Segregation of roles may happen to identify frauds that have occurred in some circumstances, but its primary role is to prevent fraud as it would require collusion between multiple members of staff. Statement two is correct – general controls are designed to ensure that IT systems are operating correctly.

190 B

There should be a division of responsibilities for authorising or initiating a transaction, the physical custody and control of assets involved, and recording the transaction.

191 A

Restricting users to read-only access of key folders on the internal network aims to prevent unauthorised changes being made to the files in these folders.

192 C

Validity involves checking that the information is valid (i.e. that it is possible data). For example, it could check the birth date given for the customer and ensure it is a valid age. This is not demonstrated by the computer system in the scenario.

193 A and B

Options C is an information processing control, which focus on whether information inputted into the system is correct or not. Options A and B are general controls which check that the IT system is operating correctly and meeting their objectives.

194 A

The presence of a supervisor may deter people from committing fraud, such as taking money out of the till. B and C are examples of detective controls whereas D is an example of a corrective control.

195 B

Remember that it is the management's responsibility to ensure that the organisation has proper accounting records and true and fair financial statements. This would usually involve the company having internal controls.

196 A

Statement (ii) is incorrect as this issue of independence would normally be an issue for internal auditors – not external auditors. Statement (iv) is also incorrect as, if the internal controls are reliable, it will reduce the amount of substantive testing that the external auditor is required to perform.

197 D

Physical controls also include access controls, key-locked cabinets, CCTV and so on.

198 B

By definition.

199 B

If an organisation's internal controls are strong, it will reduce the amount of substantive testing that the external auditor will need to undertake.

FRAUD, FRAUDULENT BEHAVIOUR AND THEIR PREVENTION IN BUSINESS

200

	Yes	No
Motivation	✓	
Opportunity	✓	

The other prerequisite is dishonesty. An honest employee is unlikely to commit fraud even if given the opportunity and motive.

201 B

The fraudster hopes that no one will notice or bother to investigate the small differences individually, although in aggregate they can total a worthwhile sum.

202 D

This fraud is covered up by mis-posting future receipts to the accounts which earlier had not been credited.

This fraud is often uncovered when the perpetrator takes a holiday and is unable to make the necessary mis-postings to cover their tracks.

203 B

These transactions are often reversed out after the year-end.

Typically, sales made just before the year-end are the subject of inflated invoices which are corrected by the issue of credit notes in the New Year.

204 D

An example is a two-year lease of a building. Under current accounting practices you do not have to show the asset or the related obligation to pay the rental amounts on the balance sheet. However, you have the use of the asset and a contractual obligation to pay the rentals.

205 D

In practice many organisations find that fraud is impossible eradicate. With regards to error, as it is unintentional, it will be hard to prevent such mistakes from taking place.

In addition, there is an implied duty within an employment contract so as to encourage staff to be honest and report any actual or suspected fraud.

206 C

The auditors' primary concern is to establish whether the accounts give a true and fair view. Only if the incident of fraud was material in value, and it is not properly reflected in the financial statements, would the auditors need to issue a modified opinion on the financial statements i.e. the opinion would not say the accounts show a true and fair view.

207 C

People living beyond their means are often driven to make up the shortfall of money necessary to support such a luxury lifestyle by committing fraud.

208 C

The Nominated Officer is responsible for investigating any large or unusual transactions. They would only be reported to the appropriate authorities if there were sufficient grounds for suspicion.

209 B

Money laundering legislation can be applied to any assets obtained by criminal means.

210 B

The offences recognised are laundering, failure to report and tipping off. Placement, layering and integration are the stages of money laundering itself.

211 D

Effective teeming and lading requires access to both parts of a control cycle such as sales and receipts or purchases and payments.

212 D

This is a classic example of a Ponzi scheme (or a pyramid scheme).

213 C

Management authorisation will decrease the chances of fraudulent and inaccurate payments being made to non-existent payables.

LEADERSHIP, MANAGEMENT AND SUPERVISION

214 D

Harry's position is clearly unfavourable, with little power and a poor relationship with his staff. Psychologically distant leaders favour formal roles and relationships, judge subordinates on the basis of performance and are primarily task oriented. This would best for Harry.

In contrast psychologically close leaders do not seek to formalise roles and relationships and are more concerned with maintaining good relationships at work. Their style works best when the situation is moderately favourable.

215 B

Managers cannot delegate responsibility to more junior members of staff.

216 A

By definition.

217 C

This definition best captures the key elements of a supervisor's responsibilities, which are primarily concerned with planning and controlling the work of their group.

218 D

The focus of Taylor's model is that staff members should be scientifically chosen to ensure they are suitable for the job they are being hired to do. Once hired, management are responsible for all key decisions and providing instructions to workers. While co-operation between workers and managers should be close, scientific management does not suggest employee suggestion schemes.

219 A

Power is not conferred by the organisation, so it cannot be delegated, it must be possessed. Responsibility is not delegated. The superior, Adam, makes the subordinate, Helen, responsible to him for the authority he has delegated, but the Adam remains responsible for it to his own boss.

220 C

In Mintzberg's view, these are the ten skills managers need to develop greater effectiveness. The ten skills are as follows: Interpersonal – Figurehead, Leader, Liaison. Informational – Monitor, Disseminator, Spokesperson. Decisional – Entrepreneur, Disturbance handler, Resource allocator, Negotiator.

221 A

By definition. Note that (4) is incorrect as responsibility cannot be delegated.

222 D

Co-ordinating looks at ensuring that all staff work together (i.e. increasing goal congruence).

223 A and C

Staff bonuses mean that the manager is offering her staff a reward for adopting the system. She is also relying on referent power by using her charisma/relationship with her employees.

224 B

The grid measures concern for production on the horizontal axis and concern for people on the vertical axis. A 1.9 manager has the lowest production score on the horizontal axis (little work is achieved), but the highest people score on the vertical axis (the manager is attentive to the needs of people).

225 C

Tells = Autocratic; Sells = Persuasive; Consults = Participative; Joins = Democratic.

226 A

Statement 2 is the definition of 'style' theories.

INDIVIDUAL, GROUP AND TEAM BEHAVIOUR

227 D

Role conflict refers to the situation when there is a clash between the roles, such as the role of the employee and role of good auditor.

228 B

Role signs are visible indications of a role, such as styles of dress. Note that 'role definition' is not a key term in role theory.

229

Statement	True	False
Assertive behaviour often leads to conflict within an organisation.		✓
Individuals usually join informal groups on a voluntary basis.	✓	

Assertive behaviour involves direct, honest and professional communication. It is aggressive behaviour that violates another person's rights and often leads to additional conflict.

230 A

Teams tend to be slower at making decisions than individuals, as there are more people involved in the decision-making process. This also means that decisions are often compromises when made in teams. However, the involvement of more people in the decision making process means that teams have better control – there are a number of people to review the decisions being made.

231 D

Remember that teams are formal groups. They will be committed to achieving certain targets or objectives. The employees in the scenario are meeting informally for social reasons and are unlikely to be formally committed to the group. Note that options B and C could apply to either groups or teams.

232 A

The other six roles are Monitor-evaluator; Resource investigator; Company worker; Team worker; Finisher and Expert.

233 C

The plant role is played by a creative individual; the monitor-evaluator is good at making accurate judgements, whereas the team worker looks after the atmosphere within the team.

234 B

This is a conflict stage when people start to withdraw their cooperation and therefore jobs are not completed to the expected standard.

235 C

Dorming refers to the danger that the team will be operating on automatic pilot. Tuckman's first four stages are Forming; Storming; Norming and Performing.

236 B

Norming establishes the norms under which the group will operate. This includes how the group will take decisions, behaviour patterns, levels of trust and openness and individual roles.

237 D

The fact that the group has diverse backgrounds may well prove to be an advantage as they will be able to generate a wider range of ideas and bring a variety of skills to the team, improving overall effectiveness.

238 B

The indicators in the prompt that confirm Louis as a completer-finisher include the phrases 'keen eye for detail', identifies minor details in documents that others miss', 'always meets his deadlines' and 'reluctant to involve others'. These are consistent with Belbin's descriptions of the contributions that the completer-finisher can make, as well as possible weaknesses.

Like the completer-finisher, the implementer (or company worker) is disciplined and reliable but is typified by being prepared to take concepts and ideas and then put them into practical effect. The monitor-evaluator considers all alternatives and often displays good judgement, but may lack personal drive. The shaper is good under pressure and challenges the team to achieve its goals.

239 A and B

Options C and D are incorrect – Peters and Waterman argued that teams should have a limited duration, existing only to achieve a given task and that communication should be unstructured and informal. In addition, they argued that successful teams need to be action-oriented.

MOTIVATING INDIVIDUALS AND GROUPS

240 C

The work of office staff is usually hard to quantify, however they have a significant influence on the income a company generates and therefore it is presumed that they should share a part of the profit.

241 A

According to Herzberg, career progression and the status increase that goes with this can act as a motivator.

242 A

In the short run you can have one without the other, but in the long run there is usually congruence.

243 B

This would meet the need for recognition and status. If an employee is concerned about the loss of their home, they are being motivated by 'basic' needs. Challenging work would fall into Maslow's 'self-fulfilment' category, while regular staff parties would motivate staff members in the 'social' category.

244 C

Large pay rises are a classic 'ego' factor. Pension schemes and permanent contracts will give the employee security, while covering living (or essential) costs is a basic need.

245 C

This allows people to grow personally and professionally by exposing them to higher levels of responsibility and more challenging tasks.

246 B and C

A would be appropriate to Theory X workers, who must be coerced to get them to make an effort.

For Theory Y workers, a participative, liberating, developmental approach would be appropriate.

247 A

Such people are seen as lazy and will work only if there is a direct link between efforts and rewards.

248 B

This is the definition of hygiene factors.

249 C

A and B are examples of self-fulfilment, while D is a security (or safety) level factor.

250 A

Piecework means that employees are paid for each unit they produce. The pay system will therefore tend to encourage staff to produce units as quickly as possible – potentially leading to poor quality. They should therefore be encouraged to ensure the quality of their work is high.

LEARNING AND TRAINING AT WORK

251

This would be an example of informal learning for the trainee accountant.

Mentoring is an example of informal learning – which is deliberate but not highly structured. Other examples of informal learning include self-directed learning and networking.

252 C

Learning includes the acquisition of a new skill, new knowledge, a modified attitude or a combination of all three.

253 C

The others are: toleration of risk and failure as well as a systematic approach to problem-solving

254 D

Divergent is a style of learning, while the others are the stages in the learning process.

255

	Pragmatist	**Reflector**	**Activist**
J dislikes reading instruction booklets and prefers a hands-on approach to learning.			✓
H learns by watching others undertake a task first, before trying to imitate them.		✓	

Activists prefer to learn through doing. Reflectors prefer observational learning activities.

256 B

While Kolb argues that there are four stages to the learning process, they form a cycle which can be started at any stage.

257 A

By definition.

258 A

Activists are learners that need a constant inflow of new ideas. They are constantly searching for new challenges and are likely to be exposed to such experiences when interacting with a group.

259 D

A is a theorist, B is a reflector and C is an activist.

260 B

According to Kolb, people who have a clear learning style preference, for whatever reason, will tend to learn more effectively if learning is geared to their preference.

261

Definition	**Training**	**Education**	**Development**
'The activities which aim at developing skills, values and understanding required in all aspects of life.'		✓	
'The growth or realisation of a person's ability and potential through conscious or unconscious learning.'			✓

262 C

By definition.

263 C

Review of staff performance and aspirations can be used to identify possible training and development opportunities in the future.

REVIEW AND APPRAISAL OF INDIVIDUAL PERFORMANCE

264 A

Julian has had targets set, but his manager has failed to monitor his performance through the year and provide regular feedback.

265 B

The decision to terminate an employee would not normally be taken at an annual appraisal (except under unusual circumstances).

266 B

Assessment criteria may include quantitative issues, such as volume of work produced or qualitative issues, such as personal skills of work quality.

267 A

Succession planning refers to preparing the next generation of managers. Appraisal helps to identify the strengths and weaknesses of an individual employee and helps to map the path to taking on a more senior role.

268 A

Ali is trying to persuade Hans that the appraisal is fair and that he should agree with her recommendations. Communication is one way.

269 D

Discharge could be as a result of an employee's unsuitability, disciplinary action or redundancy. Unavoidable may be because of marriage, moving house, illness or death. Avoidable is often due to pay, working conditions or relationships with work colleagues.

270 A

This is an example of discharge as Mary is being dismissed. 'Avoidable' would involve issues with pay or conditions, while 'unavoidable' would include illness or death.

271 B

One should divide the total number of employees leaving the organisation (or the total replacements) by the average number in the workforce.

272 D

Appraisals do not have to be formal to be effective. The final 'F' is fair.

PERSONAL EFFECTIVENESS AT WORK

273 D

This task will become more urgent over the next few weeks

274 D

An established job with set routines should make it easier for Javier to manage his time, as should having a closed-door policy which discourages time-wasters. Having Javier's colleagues in the same office will reduce travelling time and will not be a barrier to time management. However, if Javier finds it difficult to be assertive, he may struggle to deal with colleagues who waste his time.

275 B

The definition given for intranets is actually that of email. Intranets are internal networks that allow employees to access a central store of information.

276 C

Competency frameworks look at skills, knowledge and attitudes needed – not necessarily qualifications.

277 D

Counselling is about helping people to help themselves; it helps people to address their worries and anxieties created by relationships, uncertainty or problems within the individual themself.

Counselling is also non-directive; the individual is to decide themself what is to be achieved and the best ways to do so.

278

Definition	Mentoring	Coaching	Counselling
'The process of offering help, guidance and advice to facilitate the learning and development of another.'	✓		
'Helping another individual to identify and deal with a problem or problems.'			✓

279 B

This would be the role of a mentor.

280 B

Tasks should always be prioritised based on the business impact/importance.

281 D

Being effective means getting the result that you want.

There are a variety of planning aids (e.g. electronic personal organisers and hand-held computerised diaries) to support and improve personal productivity.

282 B

The goal of a PDP is to develop the individual themselves.

283 A

They should be SMART – specific, measurable, achievable/attainable, relevant and timely/time-constrained.

284 A

Suppression involves the manager threatening the conflicting employees with punishment, reduction involves negotiating a settlement and resolution involves solving the problem that is the root cause of the conflict.

285 D

Resolution involves solving the problem that is causing the conflict. In this case, Omar has little or no control over access to IT staff, so he is unlikely to be able to resolve the conflict. Denial and suppression tend to be short-term solutions – given that Omar needs a longer term solution, negotiation or reduction would be the most appropriate.

286 A

Make sure that you can identify standard consequences of employee ineffectiveness at work, such as reduced motivation, quality and communication.

COMMUNICATING IN BUSINESS

287 D

A grapevine network connects people who have a common interest and usually circulates rumours and gossip.

Also, Research has established that only 10% of the message is communicated through words, the other 90% is transmitted through non-verbal communication.

288 A

Most companies can produce such examples of instructions, control reports, etc which are distributed on the basis of seniority or status. If information is regularly sent out to a set list of people, many of them may find that the information provided is not relevant to them.

289 B

Barriers to communication also include anything that stops information from being understood by its recipients or being acted upon in the way intended.

Barriers to communication can be caused by many things, e.g. 'noise' (message confused by extraneous matters); difference in education levels; overload (too much information); distortion of information by the receiver; use of technical or professional language.

290 B

Lateral is another name for horizontal communication, within a committee people from different functions come together to present their view on an issue.

291 C

Options A and B tend to be problems when lateral communication is lacking as this means that management team members are failing to communicate with each other adequately. Option D tends to be an issue when downwards communication is lacking (i.e. managers don't communicate with junior staff members). If junior members of staff are unable to communicate upwards (i.e. to their managers) there will, however, be a lack of participation in decision-making, which may lead to a fall in motivation.

292 D

The communication has been made too late – after work has begun. This will lead to lost time and money for the business.

293 A

Information overload is one of the barriers to communication; it makes it difficult to prioritise.

294 C

The wheel was shown to be the quickest way to reach a conclusion.

295 D

Under time pressure the all-channels system either restructures (to form a wheel) or disintegrates.

296 B

The all-channel is the most likely process to reach the best decision.

297 C

Diagonal communication is between individuals or groups at different levels of the hierarchy and in different departments or functions. A is an example of vertical communication, while B and D are examples of lateral communication.

298 B

The wheel has a central individual who controls the flow of communication.

Section 4

ANSWERS TO MULTI-TASK QUESTIONS – SECTION B

THE BUSINESS ORGANISATION AND ITS EXTERNAL ENVIRONMENT

1 (a)

Stakeholder	**Internal**	**Connected**
Employees	✓	
Shareholders		✓
Customers		✓
Directors	✓	

(b) (i) F Co is partly owned by H, who is considered to have high power and low interest. F Co has therefore decided to use a **keep satisfied** strategy to manage this stakeholder.

(ii) F Co is aware that its actions are regularly commented on by HHH, which would be classified by Mendelow as **keep informed**. HHH has a high level of interest, but low power.

2

Stakeholder	**A**	**B**	**C**	**D**
Customers			✓	
Government	✓			
Shareholders		✓		
Employees				✓

3 (a) **A, D, F** and **H**

(b) (i) **A**

(ii) **D**

(iii) **C**

(iv) **B**

4 (a) **C, D, F** and **G** are correct.

(b) (i) BVO has noted that product Y's sales have fallen in recent years due to a fall in disposable income of its major customers. This is evidence that **a shift** in the demand curve for the product has occurred.

(ii) BVO sells product Z in country G. Only one other manufacturer sells a similar product in country G, meaning that the two companies dominate the market. Currently, production and sales volumes for these products has reached exactly the same levels, suggesting **equilibrium** in the market for this product.

5 (a)

Issue	**Delayering**	**Downsizing**	**Outsourcing**
Could allow third party organisations access to Y's information and processes, leading to loss of competitive advantage.			✓
Keeping the current management structure, but reducing the number of staff could lead to demotivation among the remaining workers.		✓	
Eliminating several levels of unnecessary management to reduce Y's costs, leading to lower prices for customers.	✓		
This is likely to lead to a more 'team-working' approach, where employees take on different roles in different teams, as necessary.	✓		

(b) (i) Y is considering outsourcing some of its call centre activities to GH Co. GH will provide **partial** outsourcing, with GH operators taking calls from new customers looking to purchase a policy. Y's existing staff will deal with existing customer renewals, queries and complaints.

(ii) Y has been approached by another company, HG Co, which has offered to provide extra call centre staff in the month of January – which is the busiest time of year for Y. This **ad hoc** outsourcing would help Y to avoid losing customers due to the long delays customers can face on the phone during this month.

6

Issue	**A**	**B**	**C**	**D**	**E**	**F**	**G**	**H**	**I**	**J**
MBV's employees are heavily unionised, making it difficult for the company to change their terms and conditions.					✓					
MBV's products are sold through two main retail chains in country G. Each retailer sells approximately equal amounts of MBV's furniture.			✓							
MBV is much larger than any other fine furniture manufacturers in country G, which has given it an advantage due to significant economies of scale. MBV still retails its products at a similar price to its rivals.								✓		
The market for fine furniture in country G is growing very slowly.		✓								

7 (a) (i) A

(ii) D

(iii) B

(iv) None

(v) C

(b) **B, D** and **E** are correct.

8 (a)

	Cyclical	**Real wage**	**Structural**	**Frictional**
Tends to occur in industries that are highly unionised.		✓		
Caused by aggregate demand in the economy being too low to create employment opportunities.	✓			
Short-term unemployment as people move between jobs.				✓
Caused by changes in the skills required by the economy.			✓	

(b) (i) Management of the Government's taxation and spending plans is known as **fiscal policy**.

(ii) Poor economic growth over an extended period can sometimes lead to rises in the prices of goods and services. This is referred to as **stagflation**.

9 (a) **A, B, D** and **G** are correct.

(b)

	Operations	**Outbound logistics**	**Service**	**Procurement**
POL has a small call centre dedicated to dealing with customer complaints.			✓	
Water is filtered through a four-stage process before being purified and bottled.	✓			
POL's purchasing department regularly shops around to get the lowest possible price for POL's glass bottles from suppliers.				✓
Bottled water is held in large warehouses before being transported to retailers across country H.		✓		

ORGANISATIONAL STRUCTURE, CULTURE, GOVERNANCE AND SUSTAINABILITY

10 (a)

	Hollow	**Virtual**	**Modular**
Internal functions that give competitive advantage to the company are outsourced to third parties.		✓	
The manufacturing of some components of the company's product are outsourced to third parties.			✓
Only non-core functions are outsourced to third parties.	✓		
The organisation only exists as a network of contracts.		✓	

(b) (i) W Co is partly owned by Z, a **public limited company** that has recently sold a large number of its shares on the open market in order to raise finance.

(ii) W Co is aware that its actions are regularly commented on by VVV, which is a **non-governmental organisation**. VVV campaigns for fair banking and has recently been granted charitable status.

11 (a)

	Strategic	Operational	Tactical
PASS's office managers have started detailed planning of shift patterns for all PASS tutors.		✓	
PASS is considering the acquisition of a small, rival training company.	✓		
PASS's managers are considering offering human resource management courses as well as accountancy training.	✓		
PASS's managers have decided to increase the number of staff in one particular PASS office.			✓

(b) **D, E, F and H** are correct.

12 (a) **B, C, E** and **F** are correct.

(b)

	Penetration pricing	Going rate pricing	Cost plus pricing	Price skimming
The toys could be launched at a low initial price to gain market share and then the price is raised later to maximise profits.	✓			
The toys are fairly innovative, so GRR may launch them at a high price and then drop them to a lower level later when its rivals launch similar products.				✓
GRR may sell its toys at the same price as similar rival products to ensure it is able to compete successfully.		✓		
GRR could sell the products at a 15% mark-up.			✓	

13 (i) F

(ii) L

(iii) G

(iv) C

14 (a)

	Power	Person	Task	Role
Typically a bureaucratic organisation.				✓
Often found in owner-managed organisations.	✓			
The culture exists to satisfy the needs of particular individuals.		✓		
People usually describe their position in terms of the results they are achieving.			✓	

(b) **A, C, F and H** are correct.

15 (a)

Statement	**True**	**False**
Audit committees are responsible for reviewing accounting policies and ensuring they are appropriate.	✓	
Remuneration committees should be made up of two or more non-executive directors if the company is small.	✓	
The nominations committee helps the company to select which of the nominated audit firms should be selected by the company.		✓
Both internal and external auditors report to the audit committee.	✓	

(b) **B, C, F and G** are correct.

16 (a) **A, D, E** and **G** are correct.

(b) (i) 'The **nomination** committee is responsible for ensuring that there is an appropriate mix of skills and experience on the board, as well as making sure there are sufficient non-executive directors.'

(ii) 'Wholly staffed by non-executive directors, the **audit** committee reviews systems of internal control as well as reviewing the accounting policies of the company.'

BUSINESS FUNCTIONS, REGULATIONS AND TECHNOLOGY

17 (a)

Information	**Strategic**	**Operational**
Long-term focus	✓	
Highly detailed		✓
Produced frequently		✓
Mainly an internal focus		✓

(b) (i) 'PPR has a till system which records each sale made through the day. At the end of the day, this **transaction processing system** summarises all the information on sales for the day and produces a report.'

(ii) 'PPR's **expert system** enables us to quickly calculate our tax bill for the year. We have complex rules we need to follow with this calculation and they are all pre-programmed into this system.'

18 (a) **A, C, E** and **G** are correct.

(b) (i) B

(ii) C

(iii) A

(iv) D

19 (a)

	Management accounting	**Financial accounting**
Preparation of the statement of profit or loss		✓
Recording of business transactions		✓
Preparation of statements for K Co's internal use	✓	
No legal formats used	✓	

(b) (i) '**Equity** is the best way of raising external finance for K, as it never has to be repaid by the company.'

(ii) 'K has recently entered into a scheme that will reduce its tax bill significantly. It is believed that, while legal, it is designed to defeat the tax laws laid down by the Government. As such, it is classified as a **tax avoidance** scheme.'

20 (a)

	SOPL	**SOFP**	**SOCF**
Shareholders' equity		✓	
Total cash spent purchasing non-current assets			✓
Gross margin	✓		
Administrative expenses	✓		

(b) (i) D

(ii) B

(iii) C

(iv) A

21 (a) **B, C, D** and **E** are correct.

(b) The correct order is **C, A, B, D**.

22 (a) (i) D

(ii) C

(iii) B

(iv) A

(b) **A, C, D** and **G** are correct.

23 (a) **A, C, D** and **F** are correct.

(b) **B, C, G** and **H** relate to internal audit

24 (a) **A, B, E** and **G** are correct.

(b) (i) 'For BFG, I have concerns about our **control environment**, as the senior managers take little notice of our control systems and don't seem to see them as important.'

(ii) 'There are some areas where we lack appropriate **control activities**. In particular we need segregation of duties when dealing with cash receipts.'

25 (a) (i) D

(ii) A

(iii) B

(iv) C

(b) (i) '**Layering** involves transferring money between businesses or locations in order to conceal their original source.'

(ii) 'Recently, a criminal used stolen cash to buy shares in a company. This is an example of **placement**.'

26 (a) **C, D, E** and **H** are correct.

(b)

	Board of Directors	**Audit Committee**	**All employees generally**
Ongoing monitoring and review of internal control and risk management systems.		✓	
Maintaining sound systems of internal control.	✓		
An implied duty to report suspected fraud to their superiors.			✓
An annual review of the effectiveness of internal controls and the reporting of this to shareholders.	✓		

LEADERSHIP AND MANAGEMENT

27 (a)

	Expert	**Reward**	**Referent**	**Legitimate**
FFC's Chair				✓
FFC's Coach	✓			
FFC's CEO		✓		
FFC's advisory coach			✓	

(b) (i) FFC's CEO has shown a lack of **management** as he/she has not ensured that FFC's resources have been well co-ordinated to maximise the strength of the team, while still having sufficient cash reserves to undertake all other necessary activities.

(ii) FFC's coach has shown excellent **supervision** skills. He/she has therefore been given responsibility for planning and controlling the actions of the team. He/she has improved the number of matches the team has won and has provided advice and support where necessary.

28 (a) (i) A4

(ii) A1

(iii) A2

(iv) A3

(b) (i) C

(ii) B

(iii) D

(iv) A

29 (a) The correct answers are: **A, B** and **E**

(b) (i) B

(ii) D

(iii) C

(iv) E

(v) A

30 (a) (i) D

(ii) A

(iii) B

(iv) C

(b) The correct statements are: **B, D, G** and **H.**

31 (a) (i) C

(ii) D

(iii) A

(iv) B

(b) The correct statements are: **A, B, C** and **D.**

32 (a) **B, C, D** and **H** are correct.

(b) (i) A

(ii) D

(iii) B

(iv) C

33 (a) **A, E, G** and **H** are correct.

(b) The correct statements are **B, C, E** and **F**.

34 (a) The correct order is: **B, D, C, E, A**

(b) The correct statements are: **A, D and E**

35 (i) Samuel is considering the launch of a new policy that ensures that all members of staff are given an appropriate level of pay by formalising the grade boundaries of all staff. This will make pay fairer and will act as a **hygiene factor** for workers, hopefully reducing staff turnover.

(ii) Samuel has informed all managers within UHPD that they will be expected to delegate some responsibility down to more capable junior staff to improve UHPD's employee job design. Samuel referred to this in his report as **job enrichment**.

(iii) Samuel has identified four managers within UHPD that have received high levels of complaints from their staff. They have adopted an authoritarian management style, assuming that employees are **Theory X**. In fact, this is not the case and this mismatch in style has caused significant morale problems.

(iv) Samuel has decided against **job rotation** within UHPD as he is concerned that if staff are regularly moved between departments, their overall efficiency will drop.

36 (a) (i) A

(ii) D

(iii) B

(iv) C

(b)

	Training	**Education**	**Development**
Defined as the activities which develop knowledge and skills for all aspects of life, rather than just a single job or task.		✓	
Helping the individual to grow towards current and future roles within the organisation.			✓
Helps an individual carry out their work effectively.	✓		
Tends to be job-oriented rather than personalised.	✓		

PERSONAL EFFECTIVENESS AND COMMUNICATION IN BUSINESS

37 (a) The correct order is: **C, B, D, A**

(b) The correct statements are **B, C, D** and **H**.

38 (a)

Role	**Coach**	**Mentor**
Giving general guidance and help to Emir.		✓
Improving Emir's skills on a particular machine.	✓	
Acting as an impartial sounding board for any problems Emir might have.		✓
Has a defined time period in which it should be completed.	✓	

(b) (i) Emir was in conflict with an existing employee, Oscar. The manager decided that the conflict was not significant enough to get involved and took no action, adopting a **denial** approach.

(ii) Emir was also in conflict with another new employee, Leon. This was found to be because Leon was being paid more than Emir in spite of having equivalent experience and qualifications. The manager adopted a **resolution** strategy and increased Emir's pay accordingly.

39 (a) The correct answers are: **A, C, E** and **G**.

(b)

Activity	**Analysis of Thomas's current position**	**Action plan**	**Goal setting**
Ensuring that all objectives set for Thomas are measurable.			✓
Carrying out a personal SWOT analysis for Thomas.	✓		
Set specific targets for Thomas to work towards, along with details of how success will be measured.		✓	
Identifying that Thomas has poor time management skills.	✓		

40 (a) The correct answers are: **A, D, E** and **F**.

(b) (i) D

(ii) B

(iii) C

(iv) A

PROFESSIONAL ETHICS

41 (a) The correct answers are: **B, C, F** and **G**.

(b) (i) An accountant previously suggested a new strategy to an organisation he/she prepares the accounts for. He/she has since been asked to examine the strategy to see if it has been a success. He/she therefore faces a major **self-review** threat to his/her professional ethics.

(ii) An accountant has been asked to work on the accounts for an organisation that is currently managed by his wife, exposing him to a threat of **familiarity**.

42 (a) The correct answers are: **A, B, F** and **H.**

(b) (i) Company W has decided to press ahead with plans to open a new factory. It will have a detrimental effect on the environment and the local residents, but will make the company a significant profit. The company has therefore adopted an **egoism** approach to ethics.

(ii) If company W decided to redesign the factory in order to minimise the impact on the residents and environment, but still make an overall (though lesser) profit than before, its approach to ethics would now be **pluralism**.

43 (a) The correct answers are: **D, E, F** and **H.**

(b) (i) Zeinab is a qualified accountant. She has recently faced an ethical threat of self-review. If she does nothing to deal with this, she will have breached her requirement to act with **objectivity**.

(ii) Eden has recently been undertaking an audit on KJH Co and has discovered that the company is paying its employees lower than the legal minimum wage. Reporting this information is not a breach of **confidentiality** as there is a legal reason to do so.

Section 5

PRACTICE SIMULATION QUESTIONS

SECTION A – ALL 46 questions are compulsory and MUST be attempted

1 Which of the following statements is true?

A Partnerships offer the same benefits to investors as limited companies

B Sole traders have no personal liability for business debts

C Limited companies are classed as a separate legal entity; therefore the shareholders are not personally liable for any debts of the business

D A partnership can be made up of no more than 20 partners **(2 marks)**

2 J Ltd is planning to sell a range of products that are tailored specifically to women between the ages of 20 and 30 who have children. Which of Porter's generic strategies has J adopted?

A Cost leadership

B Focus

C Differentiation **(1 mark)**

3 According to Fiedler, which of the following are true of psychologically close managers?

(i) They tend to be reserved in their relationships with subordinates.

(ii) They prefer to seek staff opinions informally rather than use formal consultation methods.

(iii) They are primarily people-orientated

A (i) and (ii)

B (ii) and (iii)

C (iii) only

D (i) only **(2 marks)**

4 Mintzberg identified ten managerial roles. Which of these managerial roles transmits factual and value based information to subordinates?

A Liaison

B Monitor

C Disseminator

D Spokesperson **(2 marks)**

5 If a government increased its expenditure and reduced levels of taxation the effect would be to reduce/stimulate/increase* demand in the economy and to reduce/stimulate/increase* the size of the Public Sector Net Cash Requirement (PSNCR).

Which words correctly complete this statement?

*delete as appropriate **(2 marks)**

6 A profession does not need to have a distinct ethical code unless this is required by statute.

Is this statement true or false?

A True

B False **(1 mark)**

7 Lo-cost Ltd offers its employees the following conditions as part of their employment:

(i) Competitive salaries

(ii) Training programmes

(iii) Safe and pleasant working conditions

(iv) Considerate supervision

According to Herzberg's two-factor theory of motivation, which of the above factors will motivate employees in the long run to become more productive?

A (i), (ii) and (iii)

B (i) only

C (i), (ii) and (iv)

D (ii) only **(2 marks)**

8 **In relation to organisational structures which of the following is the correct definition of the phrase 'span of control'?**

A The number of employees that a manager is directly responsible for

B The number of management levels in an organisational structure

C The number of levels in the hierarchy below a given manager

D The number of managers in the organisation **(2 marks)**

9 **Javier has recently been asked to join the board of HH Co as a non-executive director. Which of the following is likely to impair his independence as a non-executive director?**

A He retired from a managerial role in HH Co 7 years ago

B He holds a very small number of shares in HH Co

C He is a member of HH Co's corporate pension scheme **(1 mark)**

10 Classify the following as either internal, external or connected stakeholders.

Stakeholders	**Internal**	**External**	**Connected**
Government			
Shareholders			

(2 marks)

11 Which of the following is an example of cyclical unemployment?

A Lay-offs among ski instructors in the summer months

B Automation of ticket sales at train stations resulting in the redundancy of ticket officers

C Recession, leading to a fall in demand within the building industry

D The restriction of employment in the car industry due to a powerful trade union keeping wages high **(2 marks)**

12 Which of the following factors could influence the culture of an organisation?

(i) Past successes and failures experienced by the organisation

(ii) Senior management

(iii) The person who founded the organisation

(iv) The technology used by the organisation

(v) The industry the organisation in

A (i), (iii) and (iv)

B (i), (ii), (iii) and (iv)

C (ii), (iii) and (v)

D (i), (ii), (iii), (iv) and (v) **(2 marks)**

13 In relation to the management of conflict, which of the following approaches will most likely be effective at dealing with major conflicts between staff members who will need to continue working together in the long term?

A Negotiation

B Denial

C Suppression **(1 mark)**

14 Consider the following benefits:

1 Improved succession planning

2 Increased motivation

3 Reduced labour costs

Which of these would likely to be achieved by the use of job enrichment?

A 1 and 2 only

B 2 and 3 only

C 1, 2 and 3 **(1 mark)**

15 An item of produce is described as having an 'inelastic' demand. What is its price elasticity of demand likely to be?

A Less than 1

B Equal to 1

C Greater than 1

D Negative **(2 marks)**

16 In an organisation which operates a good system of corporate governance, to whom should the internal audit department of an organisation report?

A The Board of Directors

B The Finance Director

C The Audit Committee

D The Management Accountant **(2 marks)**

17 Which of the following is delegated to a subordinate by a superior?

A Responsibility

B Authority

C Power **(1 mark)**

18 Porter's five forces model identifies external factors that determine the potential profitability and therefore attractiveness of a particular industry. Which of the following is one of these forces?

A Bargaining power of buyers

B Government regulation of the industry

C Fiscal policy

D Technological innovation **(2 marks)**

19 Country M has a large number of service industries. It has recently decided to implement minimum wage legislation, meaning that all workers are guaranteed a certain level of pay. This level has been set slightly higher than the current average wage.

Which of the following is a likely consequence of this legislation?

A A reduction in the supply of labour within country M

B An excess of labour supply (increased unemployment) within country M

C A reduction in prices charged to consumers, benefiting those on low incomes

D An increase in the quality of services offered within country M **(2 marks)**

20 _________ systems pool data from internal and external sources and make information available to senior managers for unstructured decisions.

Which word or phrase correctly completes the above sentence?

Expert/executive information/management information/decision support*

*delete as appropriate **(2 marks)**

21 **Which of the following are consequences of a failure to comply with the legal requirements of maintaining financial records?**

(i) Fines

(ii) Prosecution

(iii) Difficulties raising finance

(iv) Unqualified audit report

(v) Damaged reputation

(vi) Qualified audit report

A (i), (ii), (v) and (vi) only

B (i), (ii), (iii) and (iv) only

C (i), (ii), (iii), (iv) and (v) only

D (i), (ii), (iii), (v) and (vi) only **(2 marks)**

22 Ava works for VCF Ltd and has been asked to locate three pieces of information for her manager:

1 The total cost of making one unit of BH364 – VCF's only product

2 The total equity of the company

3 The difference between the original budget and actual results achieved in the last year

Where would Ava need to look for each of these pieces of information? Match EACH of the above pieces of information with ONE of the reports below.

- Statement of profit or loss
- Budget
- Standard cost card
- Statement of financial position
- Variance report
- Budget
- Statement of cash flows **(2 marks)**

23 Managers are said to have a financial/fiscal/fiduciary* responsibility (or duty of faithful service) to the organisations that they serve.

Which of the terms correctly completes this sentence?

*delete as appropriate **(1 mark)**

24 **A Ltd needs to make a rapid decision about the launch of a new product and is considering whether to set up a committee to investigate this. Which of the following statements is correct with regards to A's decision?**

A Committees tend to be slow at making decisions, meaning it may be inappropriate for A in this situation.

B Committees ensure that all the individuals involved are held responsible for the decision that the committee makes.

C Committee members usually attend committee meetings full time, meaning that their normal work-load may suffer. **(1 mark)**

25 **Which of the following would raise ethical issues for a manufacturer of chocolate?**

(i) The materials used in the production of the chocolate

(ii) The quality of the chocolate

(iii) How the chocolate is advertised

(iv) How much its cocoa supplier pays its staff

(v) How much it pays its own staff

A (i) and (ii)

B (i), (ii) and (iii) only

C (i), (ii), (iii) and (v) only

D (i), (ii), (iii), (iv) and (v) only **(2 marks)**

26 HGF Ltd is considering implementing a corporate social responsibility (CSR) policy. However it is concerned that there may be drawbacks to this. An employee has identified a list of possible problems caused by a CSR policy.

Identify which of the following drawbacks are correct.

	Correct	**Incorrect**
Increased materials cost		
Failure to attract and retain quality employees		

(2 marks)

27 William is considering introducing a set of formal systems within his department.

Which of the following would be an advantage of this?

A Transactions can be recorded in different ways, increasing the flexibility of the system

B Newer staff will not require training in how to record business transactions

C Best practice can be adopted by all employees, increasing efficiency

D The need for an external audit will be reduced due to the increased accuracy of the systems **(2 marks)**

28 **James has recently placed some of his earnings into a scheme which is designed to reduce the amount of tax he pays to the Government. The scheme is legal, but a Government minister has described it as 'frustrating the intentions of Parliament'. The scheme is therefore an example of:**

A Tax evasion

B Tax mitigation

C Tax avoidance **(1 mark)**

29 **Which of the following is NOT a strategy for dealing with conflict?**

A Orchestration

B Reduction

C Resolution

D Suppression **(2 marks)**

30 Overstating overtime worked is:

1 unethical

2 fraudulent.

Identify whether the following statements are true or false.

Statement	**True**	**False**
Overstating overtime worked is unethical.		
Overstating overtime worked is fraudulent.		

(2 marks)

31 Nadia has recently been asked by her manager if she wishes to attend a series of classes covering basic mathematics and computer skills. Nadia does not use these skills in her current role and is unlikely to need them in any future role she may take on within the organisation.

What are these classes an example of?

A Education

B Development

C Training **(1 mark)**

32 **Which of the following are key components of an organisation's internal control environment?**

(i) The control environment

(ii) The entity's risk assessment processes

(iii) The entity's process for monitoring of internal controls

(iv) Information systems and communication

(v) Expert systems

(vi) Automation of systems

A (i), (ii), (iii) and (iv) only

B (i), (ii), (iii) and (vi) only

C (i), (ii), (iii), (v) and (vi) only

D (i), (ii), (iii), (iv) and (vi) only **(2 marks)**

33 Valentina is the leader of a team which tends to communicate via e-mail. Team members send all messages to Valentina who checks the content of the messages and then forwards them on to the other team members if she feels they need to be made aware of any of the information.

Which communication pattern is Valentina using in her team?

A The 'Y'

B The wheel

C All channel

D The circle **(2 marks)**

34 David has just had his performance appraisal. He was told that his work was unacceptable and if he doesn't improve in the next two months he will be dismissed.

What approach was used in David's appraisal?

A Tell and sell approach

B Tell and listen approach

C Problem solving approach

D 360 degree approach **(2 marks)**

35 Competency frameworks are the critical skills, knowledge and attitudes that a job-holder must have in order to perform effectively.

Is this statement true or false?

A True

B False **(1 mark)**

36 Yan manages a small team of workers. She feels that the team do what she asks of them because she can offer them benefits, such as overtime and bonuses.

According to Bennis, what type of leader is Yan?

A Transformational

B Transactional **(1 mark)**

37 **A large management consultancy has implemented a matrix structure. Many of the consultants work in temporary project teams. Which of Handy's cultural types would you expect to see in this organisation?**

A Role Culture

B Power Culture

C Task Culture

D Person Culture **(2 marks)**

38 **In the context of audit, identify whether the following statements are true or false, in terms of what 'substantive tests' are trying to accomplish.**

Statement	**True**	**False**
To establish the causes of errors and omissions in financial records.		
To identify errors and omissions in financial records.		

(2 marks)

39 **According to Maslow's hierarchy of needs, which TWO of the following rewards might you pursue in order to have your ego/ esteem needs satisfied?**

A Being invited to join colleagues for a drink after work

B Achieving praise on an achievement from those within your team

C Opportunity to undertake further professional development

D Award of a trophy in recognition of your performance **(2 marks)**

40 Consider the following roles:

1 Providing advice and support to members of their team

2 Answering calls along with their team

3 Reporting to management on a periodic basis

Which of these roles would typically be undertaken by a supervisor?

A 1 and 2 only

B 1 and 3 only

C 1, 2 and 3 **(1 mark)**

41 Louise is an accountant working in a large company. She has just been asked by her manager to not put through a number of inaccurate invoices in order to improve the accounts.

What should Louise's first course of action be?

A Report this to a senior manager/head of ethics in her company

B Report to the ACCA

C Report to the authorities

D Resign **(2 marks)**

42 The stages of Kolb's experiential learning cycle are as follows:

1 Draw conclusions from the experience

2 Have an experience

3 Plan the next steps

4 Reflect on the experience

Which is the correct order?

A 2, 4, 1, 3

B 2, 3, 4, 1

C 2, 4, 3, 1

D 2, 3, 1, 4 **(2 marks)**

43 **Skimming schemes typically occur within the purchasing department. Is this statement true or false?**

A True

B False **(1 mark)**

44 G Ltd manufactures a product which is made of four components which are then bolted together. G is considering outsourcing the production of two of these components to an external company, though G would still assemble the final product itself.

Which of the following boundaryless structures will G most closely match if it proceeds with this arrangement?

A Hollow

B Virtual

C Modular **(1 mark)**

45 **Which of the following factors would tend to allow an organisation to develop a wide span of control?**

A Highly skilled, motivated employees

B Employees spread over a wide geographical area

C Employees undertake complex, changing tasks **(1 mark)**

46 Juliette has recently been asked to estimate the level of sales that her company will achieve if they launch a new product – the 'A1000'. She has undertaken market research which has cost a significant sum of money and concluded that there is little demand for the A1000. Due to technical difficulties, this information was provided a month after her company began investing in equipment to help it manufacture the A1000.

Which features of good quality information were missing from Juliette's market research?

A Precision

B Relevance

C Timeliness

D Low cost **(2 marks)**

SECTION B – ALL SIX questions are compulsory and MUST be attempted

1 Here are four short references to leadership theories:

A Managers can be categorised according to their level of concern for both production and people

B Managers may be either psychologically distant or psychologically close

C Leaders need to consider task, individual and group needs in order to be successful

D Managers need to focus on how to deal with possible resistance from their team

(a) Identify the description above, which is associated with EACH of the following theorists, by matching them up with A, B, C, D or None.

(i) Adair

(ii) Fiedler

(iii) Taylor

(iv) Blake and Mouton **(2 marks)**

(b) From the list below, identify TWO of Henri Fayol's functions of management.

A Planning

B Organising

C Managing

D Monitoring

E Motivating **(2 marks)**

(Total: 4 marks)

2 HJY Co is a large multinational organisation that is required to have annual audits. The company has two sets of auditors.

(a) Classify the following as features of either internal auditors or external auditors.

	Internal auditors	**External auditors**
Their main purpose is to offer advice to management about the company's internal controls.		
Management define the scope of their work.		
They must be independent of the company.		
Corporate Governance suggests that if they are not present in a listed company, the company must assess the need for them on an annual basis.		

(2 marks)

(b) Organisations can fall victim to a number of different types of fraud, including:

A Teeming and lading fraud

B Ponzi scheme

C Advance fee fraud

D Window dressing fraud

The following sentences contain gaps which specify a particular fraud from the above list.

One of HJY's employees has been discovered to have set up a _1_ which involved him/her using money from receivables to clear the balances of other receivables whose receipts he/she had already stolen.

(i) Select the correct type of fraud which appropriately fills gap 1 above.

teaming and lading fraud/Ponzi scheme/advance fee fraud/window dressing fraud*

*delete as appropriate **(1 mark)**

HJY also paid for an advertisement in a new local trade publication. It sent a cheque for £6,000 to the publication in order to secure a large full page advertisement. However, the publication was found to be fictitious and HJY lost its money – a classic example of a _2_.

(ii) Select the correct type of fraud which appropriately fills gap 1 above.

teaming and lading fraud/Ponzi scheme/advance fee fraud/window dressing fraud*

*delete as appropriate **(1 mark)**

(Total: 4 marks)

3 Porter's value chain examines the various activities that make up an organisation's operations.

(a) Which activity from Porter's value chain is being described below?

A The transformation of inputs into outputs

B Purchasing of materials as well as other resources

C How the firm is organised

D Any activities that occur after the point of sale

(i) Service. Select ONE of A, B, C or D

(ii) Operations. Select ONE of A, B, C or D

(iii) Procurement. Select ONE of A, B, C or D

(iv) Infrastructure. Select ONE of A, B, C or D **(2 marks)**

(b) According to Porter's five forces model, which TWO of the following indicate there is a low threat of new entrants to the market?

A Low capital requirements

B Patents exist on major product lines

C Access to distribution channels is not restricted

D Large numbers of suppliers of raw materials

E Low switching costs for customers

F Existing firms in the market are large

G Rapidly expanding market **(2 marks)**

(Total: 4 marks)

4 Country X is currently experiencing a significant downturn in its economy. The Government of Country X is looking at a number of policy options to try to deal with this. The Government does not currently have an overall policy to dealing with the country's issues.

(a) For each of the following, indicate whether they relate to classical, supply side or demand side economic theory.

	Classical theory	**Supply side**	**Demand side**
The Government should borrow money from the money markets and inject it into the economy.			
The Government should not interfere with the market and should let it reach its own equilibrium.			
The Government should provide worker retraining schemes.			
The Government should cut state benefits to make work more attractive.			

(2 marks)

(b) Complete the following sentences, with reference to economics theories.

_1_ inflation occurs in countries which make significant levels of purchases from foreign suppliers and where _2_.

(i) Select which ONE of the following fills Gap 1.

monetary/demand-pull/cost-push/imported*

*delete as appropriate

(ii) Select which ONE of the following fills Gap 2.

the money supply rises/the national currency weakens/the national currency strengthens*

*delete as appropriate

A demand curve may _1_ to the left or right if any of the demand conditions change, such as _2_.

(iii) Select which ONE of the following fills Gap 1.

expand/shift/contract*

*delete as appropriate

(iv) Select which ONE of the following fills Gap 2

elasticity/tastes/price/quantity*

*delete as appropriate **(2 marks)**

(Total: 4 marks)

5 Below is information on four different companies.

Company 1 enjoys very rapid decision making, but there are extremely limited opportunities for staff members to gain promotions, which many employees find de-motivating.

Company 2 has a highly flexible structure, but dual command has led to conflict between managers who have overlapping authority.

Company 3 enjoys significant economies of scale, but cannot easily cope with diversification into new products or markets.

Company 4 is split into several strategic business units – each related to a particular product that the company makes. While this has allowed the company to diversify, it has led to a lack of overall goal congruence within the company.

The following are organisational structures:

A Divisional

B Geographic

C Hollow

D Entrepreneurial

E Matrix

F Functional

G Boundaryless

H Modular

Required:

(i) Match Company 1 with ONE structure from the list above (A–H)

(ii) Match Company 2 with ONE structure from the list above (A–H)

(iii) Match Company 3 with ONE structure from the list above (A–H)

(iv) Match Company 4 with ONE structure from the list above (A–H)

(Total: 4 marks)

6 Ethics is a crucial part of operating as an accountancy professional.

(a) Which of the FOUR of the following ethical safeguards are typically put in place by professional accountancy bodies?

A Setting of professional standards

B Creation of internal business complaint procedures

C Professional monitoring and disciplinary procedures

D Ethics training for all professional accountants

E Creation of ethical cultures in organisations

F Ensuring openness and transparency between organisations and their stakeholders

G Creation of corporate governance requirements

H Creation of corporate codes of ethics **(2 marks)**

(b) Which FOUR of the following benefits would typically be expected to arise from an organisation adopting strong business ethics?

A Reassuring to investors

B Improved motivation of employees

C Significant time and cost savings for management

D Less reporting needed to external stakeholders

E Reduced need for external audit

F Attractive to customers

G Lower production costs

H Reduced risk of onerous Government legislation **(2 marks)**

(Total: 4 marks)

Section 6

ANSWERS TO PRACTICE SIMULATION QUESTIONS

SECTION A

1 C

A limited liability company is classed as a separate legal entity from its owners. The owners (shareholders) may be different to the managers (Board of Directors). A shareholder's liability is limited to their investment.

A partnership is different to a limited company in that there is no separate legal entity.

Sole traders have unlimited liability for business debts as they are classed as the same legal entity as the business.

There is no restriction on the number of partners in a partnership agreement.

2 B

The company is targeting its goods and services to a distinct group of people. This would be classified as a focus, or niche market, strategy.

3 B

Psychologically close managers tend to adopt close relations with their subordinates and therefore are people-orientated and prefer informal contact rather than more formal communication methods.

4 C

The disseminator transmits factual and value based information to subordinates.

The liaison develops and maintains a network of external contacts.

The monitor gathers internal and external information relevant to the organisation.

The spokesperson communicates to the outside world on the performance and policies of the organisation.

5 C

If a government increased its expenditure and reduced levels of taxation the effect would be to **stimulate** demand in the economy and to **increase** the size of the Public Sector Net Cash Requirement (PSNCR).

Demand would be stimulated as firms and households would have more money after tax for investment/consumption or saving. The increased public expenditure would not be covered by an increase in tax revenue and would therefore have to be financed by increasing government borrowing, the PSNCR.

6 B

In order to be classified as a profession, there must be enforced compliance with an appropriate ethical code.

7 D

According to Herzberg's theory only training is a motivator. The others are all hygiene factors – the absence of which will cause dissatisfaction but their presence will not lead to long-term motivation. Note that staff bonuses (in addition to their salaries) could be a motivator if they are used to recognise good performance.

8 A

The span of control is the number of people for whom a manager is directly responsible.

Scalar chain relates to the number of management levels within an organisation.

9 C

A non-executive director must not have been an employee of the organisation in the last five years and should not have had a **material** business interest in the company in the last three years. They should also not participate in the company's pension schemes.

10

Stakeholders	**Internal**	**External**	**Connected**
Government		✓	
Shareholders			✓

11 C

Recession is part of the business cycle when demand for output and therefore employees falls so unemployment rises.

A is an example of seasonal unemployment.

B is technological unemployment.

D is an example of real wage unemployment.

12 D

All options could influence the culture of an organisation. History and experiences allow the company to learn from past successes and failures, successes will be built on and failures not repeated. Senior management influence current objectives and ways of working. The person who founded the organisation establishes the basic assumptions and values of the organisation. The technology used and the industry both influence the way an organisation operates.

13 A

Negotiation involves coming up with a compromise where both parties get some (but not all) of what they want. This is likely to act as a long-term solution to a major conflict. Denial and suppression are both short-term solutions as they do not involve any attempt to deal with the root cause of the problem.

14 A

Job enrichment involves offering existing staff higher-level, possibly managerial level, tasks. This will not only help train the employee, making them more capable and therefore improving succession planning, but will also make them feel more valued and interested in their jobs, improving motivation. It is unlikely to reduce employee's wages and could, in fact, eventually lead to the employee demanding higher wages to compensate them for the additional work they are having to undertake.

15 A

Its price elasticity of demand (PED) would be less than one. If a product is inelastic, the number of units demanded will change more slowly than the sales price. This gives a PED of less than 1.

16 C

It is good corporate governance for an internal audit department to report to the audit committee, which should consist of non-executive directors, in order to increase their independence.

17 B

When delegating work, the superior gives the subordinate part of their authority. Responsibility is not delegated as the superior will still be responsible for the work to their own boss. Power is not conferred by the organisation so it cannot be delegated, it must be possessed.

18 A

Porter's five forces model identified the following factors that determine the attractiveness of an industry:

- Bargaining power of buyers
- Bargaining power of suppliers
- Competitive rivalry
- New entrants to the industry
- Substitute products or services

19 B

A minimum price would tend to cause an excess of supply in the market. In this case, that would tend to mean excess labour in the market – leading to higher unemployment. This is particularly likely as the minimum wage level is set above the current wage level. This may mean that businesses reduce the number of employees they hire, to maintain their profits.

20 **Executive information** systems pool data from internal and external sources and make information available to senior managers for unstructured decisions.

21 D

Fines, prosecution, difficulties raising finance, a damaged reputation and a qualified audit report are all possible consequences of compliance failure. An unqualified audit report is given when, in the auditors' opinion, the financial statements provide a true and fair impression of the financial position of the organisation.

22
1. Standard cost card
2. Statement of financial position
3. Variance report

Make sure you are able to identify the contents of the main financial and management reports produced by the accounts department.

23 Managers are said to have a fiduciary responsibility (or duty of faithful service) to the organisations that they serve.

Fiduciary means 'of trust'. All managers are accountable for their actions.

24 A

Committees often slow decision making down as they involve discussion and negotiation between all the members.

25 D

All of the above would raise ethical issues. Materials used impacts on the safety of the product. Quality is a safety issue. Advertising raises issues of truth and manipulation. The treatment and potential exploitation of labour, whether directly employed by a business or its suppliers, is also an ethical issue.

26

	Correct	**Incorrect**
Increased materials cost	✓	
Failure to attract and retain quality employees		✓

CSR is likely to attract good quality employees and should not lead to a loss of key skills within the organisation. However, goods need to be purchased from ethical sources, which may lead to a rise in their cost. It can also take up significant amounts of management time, which could have been used to increase business profits.

27 C

Formal systems will ensure that all transactions are recorded the same way. If all staff adopt the 'best practice' approach to using the system, efficiency will increase. Note that new staff will still need to be trained in how to use the system and the quality of the systems will have no bearing on whether the organisation requires an external audit or not – though it may make an audit easier and therefore cheaper!

28 C

Tax evasion is illegal. Tax avoidance is used to describe schemes that frustrate the intentions of Parliament, while tax mitigation describes schemes that do not frustrate the intentions of Parliament.

29 A

Orchestration is not a conflict management strategy – the other three are.

30

Statement	**True**	**False**
Overstating overtime worked is unethical.	✓	
Overstating overtime worked is fraudulent.	✓	

Overstating overtime is fraudulent as it is a subtle form of theft of funds from an organisation as an individual would be claiming pay for hours not worked. This would also clearly be unethical.

31 A

Education is a way of providing skills that will generally benefit a person in their general life. Training and development are both more focused on providing skills that will be needed for existing and future roles within the organisation.

32 A

The other component of internal control is 'control activities'.

33 B

In the wheel all communication goes through one central person. In the 'Y' a message works up a chain until it reaches an individual who is contact with more than one person. In the all channel, communication flows freely between members. In the circle, a message passes from one person to another.

34 A

The appraiser told David where he was going wrong but did not give any assistance or guidance to help David improve his future performance. The 'tell and listen' approach encourages input from the individual. The problem solving approach is where the appraiser and appraisee work together to identify problems and jointly find solutions. The 360 degree approach uses feedback from managers, subordinates and peers to review an individual's performance.

35 A

By definition.

36 B

Yan sees her relationship with her team as a simple transaction – she offers benefits in return for their obedience and compliance.

37 C

A task culture tends to exist in organisations whose members work in teams with a focus on results rather than processes.

A role culture suits bureaucratic organisations. A power culture is often seen in small entrepreneurial organisations where the owner-manager has all the power and control. A person culture exists in professional partnerships.

38

Statement	**True**	**False**
To establish the causes of errors and omissions in financial records.		✓
To identify errors and omissions in financial records.	✓	

Substantive tests 'substantiate' the figures in the accounts. They are used to discover whether figures are correct or complete, not why they are incorrect or incomplete.

39 B AND D

Ego/esteem needs are satisfied by recognition and respect from others.

40 C

These are all typical roles of a supervisor.

41 A

Typically such an unethical activity needs to be reported to whoever is responsible for dealing with ethical problems within the company. If Louise is unable to get a satisfactory resolution from them, she could discuss the matter with the ACCA. Resignation is normally the final resort.

42 A

This is a 'learning by doing approach'.

43 B

A skimming scheme occurs when a fraudster diverts small amounts from a large number of transactions. As such, it could occur anywhere within the organisation.

44 C

By definition. Hollow organisations outsource non-core functions, while virtual organisations outsource almost all functions – whether core or not.

45 A

A wide span of control means that each manager looks after many staff members. This is easier if the staff members are skilled and motivated as they will require little supervision. However, if staff are widely spread or have to undertake complex tasks, it will be harder for a manger to look after them meaning that the span of control will tend to narrow.

46 C

The information is relevant to the company's A1000 production. There is no evidence that the information is imprecise or that it is not cost effective – note that information does not have to be low cost to be good quality. However, as it was received AFTER production commenced, it was not timely and will therefore only be of limited usefulness.

SECTION B

1 (a) (i) C

(ii) B

(iii) None

(iv) A

(b) A, B

2 (a)

	Internal auditors	**External auditors**
Their main purpose is to offer advice to management about the company's internal controls.	✓	
Management define the scope of their work.	✓	
They must be independent of the company.		✓
Corporate Governance suggests that if they are not present in a listed company, the company must assess the need for them on an annual basis.	✓	

(b) (i) One of HJY's employees has been discovered to have set up a **teaming and lading fraud** which involved him/her using money from receivables to clear the balances of other receivables whose receipts he/she had already stolen.

(ii) HJY also paid for an advertisement in a new local trade publication. It sent a cheque for £6,000 to the publication in order to secure a large full page advertisement. However, the publication was found to be fictitious and HJY lost its money – a classic example of an **advance fee fraud.**

3 (a) (i) D

(ii) A

(iii) B

(iv) C

(b) B, F

4 (a)

	Classical theory	Supply side	Demand side
The Government should borrow money from the money markets and inject it into the economy.			✓
The Government should not interfere with the market and should let it reach its own equilibrium.	✓		
The Government should provide worker retraining schemes.		✓	
The Government should cut state benefits to make work more attractive.		✓	

(b) (i) and (ii) **Imported** inflation occurs in countries which make significant levels of purchases from foreign suppliers and where the **national currency weakens**.

(iii) and (iv) A demand curve may **shift** to the left or right if any of the demand conditions change, such as **tastes**.

5 (i) D

(ii) E

(iii) F

(iv) A

6 (a) A, C, D, G

(b) A, B, F, H

Section 7

SPECIMEN EXAM QUESTIONS

Section A – ALL 46 questions are compulsory and MUST be attempted

1 The major purpose of the International Accounting Standards Board (IASB) is to ensure consistency in __________.

Which two words complete the sentence above?

A Financial control

B Corporate reporting

C External auditing **(1 mark)**

2 According to the work of the Ashridge school of management, the leadership style that leasr acknowledges the contribution that subordinates have to make is ____________.

Which word correctly completes the sentence above?

A Authoritarian

B Autocratic

C Assertive **(1 mark)**

3 **In relation to the management of conflict, which of the following approaches will maximise the prospect of consensus?**

A Acceptance

B Negotiation

C Avoidance

D Assertiveness **(2 marks)**

4 Darragh has been appointed to the management team of a professional football club. His role includes coaching, mentoring and counselling young players who have just signed contracts with the club for the first time.

The following are his main activities:

1 Helping the young players to settle in during their first week

2 Identifying each player's key skills and encouraging them to develop new skills

3 Advising the players on addressing personal issues, such as managing their finances

4 Helping the players to anticipate opponents' reactions

Which of the following matches the correct role to carry out in each of the four activities?

A 1. Mentor 2. Counsellor 3. Coach 4. Counsellor

B 1. Mentor 2. Coach 3. Counsellor 4. Coach

C 1. Mentor 2. Coach 3. Counsellor 4. Mentor

D 1. Counsellor 2. Mentor 3. Coach 4. Counsellor **(2 marks)**

5 **In order to ensure that the policies of an organisation are consistent with the public interest, on which of the following should the directors of a company focus?**

A The long-term welfare of the shareholders

B Compliance with legal requirements and codes of governance

C The collective well-being of stakeholders **(1 mark)**

6 Martin is an experienced and fully trained shipbuilder, based in a western European city. Due to significant economic change in supply and demand conditions for shipbuilding in Martin's own country, the shipyard he worked for has closed and he was made redundant. There was no other local demand for his skills within his own region and he would have to move to another country to obtain a similar employment, and could only find similar work locally through undertaking at least a year's retraining in a related engineering field.

Which of the following describes the type of unemployment that Martin has been affected by?

A Structural unemployment

B Cyclical unemployment

C Frictional unemployment

D Marginal unemployment **(2 marks)**

7 **Which TWO of the following tasks would the accounts department be most likely to help the marketing department with?**

A Provide information on the most efficient way to manufacture a product

B To identify the maximum discounts that can be offered to customers

C Provide information about costs of distribution channels for the product

D Provide information on customer credit limits **(2 marks)**

8 **Auditors would find big data analytics most useful for which TWO of the following tasks?**

A Detecting unusual patterns in key accounting ratios

B Sampling smaller sets of accounting data

C Predicting the probability of key risks materialising

D Verifying the existence and ownership of assets and liabilities **(2 marks)**

9 The overall average age of a population in a country is directly dependent on two demographic factors: Birth rate and death rate.

Assuming equal rates of change, which of the following must lead to an overall ageing of the population?

	Birth rate	Death rate
A	Rising	Rising
B	Falling	Rising
C	Rising	Falling
D	Falling	Falling

(2 marks)

10 Gils is conducting an appraisal interview with his assistant Jill. He initially feeds back to Jill areas of strengths and weaknesses of performance but then invites Jill to talk about the job, her aspirations, expectations and problems. He adopts a non-judgemental approach and offers suggestions and guidance.

This is an example of which approach to performance appraisal?

A Tell and sell approach

B Tell and listen approach

C Problem solving approach

D 360 degree approach **(2 marks)**

11 **What is the primary responsibility of the external auditor?**

A To verify all the financial transactions and supporting documentation of the client

B To ensure that the client's financial statements are reasonably accurate and free from bias

C To report all financial irregularities to the shareholders of the client

D To ensure that all the client's financial statements are prepared and submitted to the relevant authorities on time **(2 marks)**

12 Amy works for a firm that provides accounting and auditing services to clients. Six months ago, Amy was seconded to one of the clients, PFG Co, to help with general accounting work. Amy has just been told that she is due to return to PFG Co as part of the external audit team.

Which threat to ethical behaviour is this?

A Familiarity

B Self-review

C Self-interest **(1 mark)**

13 Wasim is the Customer Services Manager in a large leisure park. The forthcoming weekend is going to be the busiest of the year, as it is a public holiday. Wasim has to cope with several absentees, leaving him short-staffed in public areas of the park. His manager has told him that he expects him to catch up with some administrative reports that were due last week. Wasim also has to arrange for six new staff to be trained, who will be arriving imminently.

In order to manage his workload most effectively, what should Wasim do?

A Prioritise the tasks in relation to the most important business outcomes

B Deal with the reports that the manager insists be prepared

C Train the new recruits

D Carry out some of the work that the absentees would normally do **(2 marks)**

14 In order to discharge their duties ethically, finance directors must ensure that the information published by their organisations provides a complete and precise view of the position of the business, without concealing negative aspects that may distort the reader's perception of its position.

This duty describes which of the following ethical principles?

A Probity

B Honesty

C Independence

D Objectivity **(2 marks)**

15 **Which of the following is a purpose of the International Federation of Accountants?**

A Agreement of legally binding financial reporting standards across all member accountancy organisations

B Prevention of international financial crimes, such as money laundering and insider dealing

C Promotion of ethical standards in all member organisations

D Development of universally applicable detailed rules to deter inappropriate behaviours **(2 marks)**

16 The following statements relate to the informal organisation.

1 Some organisations do not have an informal element.

2 The informal organisation should be considered when business decisions are made.

Which of the above statements are true?

A Statement 1 only

B Statement 2 only

C Both

D Neither **(2 marks)**

17 Neill works as the procurement manager of JL Company, a large services company.

Information provided by Neill is most relevant to which of the following elements of the marketing mix?

A Physical evidence

B Distribution (or place)

C Price

D Processes **(2 marks)**

18 **In relation to internal control procedures, which type of control is being used when a line manager approves the weekly hours worked that have been submitted by an employee?**

A Verification

B Authorisation

C Reconciliation **(1 mark)**

19 Malachi has been asked by his manager to analyse the financial accounts of ABC Company, which is bidding for a contract offered by Malachi's company in the near future. The two financial statements which he will be using as his sources are the statement of financial position and the statement of profit or loss. The information he is required to obtain is as follows:

1 The equity of the company

2 Operating profit as a percentage of revenue

3 Long-term borrowings

4 Liquidity

Which of the following correctly matches the above items of information with the financial statements in which they would be found?

	1	**2**	**3**	**4**
A	SOFP	SOPL	SOPL	SOFP
B	SOPL	SOFP	SOFP	SOPL
C	SOPL	SOFP	SOPL	SOFP
D	SOFP	SOPL	SOFP	SOFP

(2 marks)

20 Linh owns a busy restaurant. She has had complaints from regular customers about diners failing to control their noisy and unruly children, which is spoiling their dining experiences.

Which of the following courses of action would be regarded as a win-win solution to this problem for regular customers and diners?

A Setting aside a separate section of the restaurant for families with children

B Not accepting bookings from families with children

C Advising customers that the restaurant is a family restaurant before they book

D Taking no action, assuming that those who complain will always be a minority

(2 marks)

21 Which of the following is data protection legislation primarily designed to protect?

A All private individuals and corporate entities on whom only regulated data is held

B All private individuals on whom only regulated data is held

C All private individuals on whom any data is held

D All private individuals and corporate entities on whom any data is held **(2 marks)**

22 The system used by a company to record sales and purchases is an example of which of the following?

A A transaction processing system

B A management information system

C An office automation system

D A decision support system **(2 marks)**

23 The following are stakeholders of a business organisation:

1 Manager

2 Customer

3 Executive Director

4 Supplier

Which of the above are CONNECTED stakeholders?

A 1 and 2 only

B 2 and 4 only

C 2 and 3 only

D 3 and 4 only **(2 marks)**

24 In an economic environment of high price inflation, those who owe money will gain and those who are owed money will lose.

Is this statement true or false?

A True

B False **(1 mark)**

25 Company XYZ has been using role playing exercises with video recording and playback for its sales staff.

What benefits will Company XYZ expect to see from this type of training?

A Increased sales

B More efficient manufacturing saving costs

C Lower levels of bad debts

D Increased net profit **(2 marks)**

26 Renata has attended a leadership development course in which she experienced a self-analysis exercise using the Blake and Mouton managerial grid. The course leader informed her that the results suggested that Renata demonstrated a 9·1 leadership style.

What other conclusions may be drawn in relation to Renata's leadership style?

1 She maximises the involvement of her team

2 She demonstrates little concern for people in the team

3 She balances the needs of the team with the need to complete the task.

4 She is highly focused on achieving the objectives of the team.

A 1 and 2

B 2 and 4

C 1 and 4

D 2 and 3 **(2 marks)**

27 The implementation of a budgetary control system in a large organisation would be the responsibility of the internal auditor.

Is this statement true or false?

A True

B False **(1 mark)**

28 The following are duties of either internal or external auditors:

1 Confirming that the financial accounts present a true and fair view

2 Confirming that there are appropriate policies for preventing and detecting fraud

3 Confirming that the financial accounts have been prepared in accordance with legal requirements

Which of the above are the roles of an external auditor?

A 2 and 3

B 1 and 2

C 1 and 3 **(1 mark)**

29 Professional accountants must demonstrate integrity at all times.

Which of the following best describes the meaning of integrity?

A Applying consistently high moral values

B Maintaining a neutral and unbiased view on all business decisions

C Providing timely and accurate information free from errors **(1 mark)**

30 The following are either characteristics of a co-operative or of a public limited company:

1 Maximising the excess of income over expenditure not a primary objective

2 Members can vote according to the number of shares owned

3 Shares can be bought and sold through personal transactions of the members

4 All members are invited to attend the annual general meeting and participate in decisions at the meeting

Which of the above are the characteristics of public limited companies?

A 1 and 2 only

B 2 and 3 only

C 2 and 4 only

D 3 and 4 only **(2 marks)**

31 The pooling of ideas within a group of workers may mean greater efficiency than if the workers were acting as individuals.

Which of the following is the correct term for this concept?

A Compromise

B Synergy

C Interaction

D Group dynamics **(2 marks)**

32 **Which of the following statements about Blockchain is NOT correct?**

A Blockchains allow for increased transparency in the recording of business transactions

B Blockchains can be posted to a public ledger

C Blockchain transactions have an indelible record

D Blockchain information requires a greater need for the auditing of transactions **(2 marks)**

33 In a higher education teaching organisation an academic faculty is organised into courses and departments, where teaching staff report both to course programme managers and to subject specialists, depending on which course they teach and upon their particular subject specialism.

According to Charles Handy's four cultural stereotypes, which of the following describes the above type of organisational structure?

A Role

B Task

C Power

D Person **(2 marks)**

34 **Which statement describes a characteristic of an oligopolistic market?**

A In oligopoly, all suppliers charge the same price

B If an oligopolist increased prices, it would lose customers

C An oligopolist is not aware of the strategies of its competitors

D An oligopolist has a high level of influence within its market **(2 marks)**

35 Herzberg recognised two types of factors in his theory of motivation.

Which of the following is a 'motivator' according to Herzberg?

A Supervision

B Salary

C Responsibility **(1 mark)**

36 **Which of the following should be implemented in the workplace to safeguard against ethical threats and dilemmas?**

A A CPD (continuing professional development) requirement

B Quality control procedures

C Corporate governance codes

D Regulatory disciplinary procedures **(2 marks)**

37 **What is the responsibility of a Public Oversight Board?**

A The establishment of detailed rules on internal audit procedures

B The commissioning of financial reporting standards

C The creation of legislation relating to accounting standards

D The monitoring and enforcement of legal and compliance standards **(2 marks)**

38 Adrian is the manager of a call centre. Consultants have advised him that by reorganising his teams to complete highly specific tasks the call centre will be able to increase the throughput of work significantly, as well as increasing the number of sales calls made to the public. The reorganisation proposals are unpopular with many workers, who feel that their jobs will become tedious and repetitive.

The proposal to reorganise the work of the call centre utilises principles put forward by which school of management theorist?

A Drucker

B Taylor

C Fayol **(1 mark)**

39 Which of the following statements best describes a personal development plan?

A A personal development plan is a plan to develop personal skills and to meet personal objectives

B A personal development plan lists traits and standards against which individuals can be consistently and objectively assessed

C A personal development plan is a process whereby an individual is put under the guidance of an experienced employee who shows the individual how to perform tasks

(1 mark)

40 In the context of marketing, the 'four Ps' are price, promotion, ____________ and ____________.

Which TWO words correctly complete the above sentence?

1 Product

2 Positioning

3 Place

A 1 and 3

B 1 and 2

C 2 and 3 **(1 mark)**

41 Which one of the following is a potential advantage of decentralisation?

A Risk reduction in relation to operational decision-making

B More accountability at lower levels

C Consistency of decision-making across the organisation **(1 mark)**

42 FKT Company is considering the introduction of a code of ethics following media criticism of its selling practices.

Which of the following is most important when deciding on the content of the proposed code of ethics?

A The minimum acceptable standards of behaviour and conduct of employees (KEY)

B The legal requirements affecting the sales of core products and services

C The main issues of concern to customers who have made complaints

D The generally accepted standards by other companies operating in the same sector

(2 marks)

43 Ahmed is preparing his personal development plan. He is particularly concerned about how others see him.

In order to analyse this aspect of his personal development plan further, Ahmed should consider which of the following?

A Problems and strengths

B Strengths and opportunities

C Strengths and weaknesses **(1 mark)**

44 Jackie leads an established team of six workers. In the last month, two have left to pursue alternative jobs and one has commenced maternity leave. Three new staff members have joined Jackie's team.

Which one of Tuckman's group stages will now occur?

A Norming

B Forming

C Performing

D Storming **(2 marks)**

45 **In the context of fraud, 'teeming and lading' is most likely to occur in which area of operation?**

A Sales

B Quality control

C Advertising and promotion

D Despatch **(2 marks)**

46 **Which of the following statements is TRUE in relation to the marginal revenue function of a business in a perfectly competitive market?**

A It is diagonal

B It is horizontal

C It is vertical **(1 mark)**

Section B – ALL SIX questions are compulsory and MUST be attempted

1 Here are four references to the functions of management:

A Managers have three categories of role to perform: interpersonal, decisional and informational

B Planning and organising are two of the functions of management

C Management is the development of a true science of work

D The manager of a business has one basic function – economic performance

Required:

(a) Identify the description above which is associated with each of the following theorists, by selecting A, B, C, D or None.

(i) Peter Drucker

(ii) Henry Fayol

(iii) Henry Mintzberg

(iv) F W Taylor

Note: The total marks will be split equally between each part. (2 marks)

(b) Listed below are five types of leader.

A Psychologically distant leader

B Psychologically close leader

C Transactional leader

D Transformational leader

E Autocratic leader

Required:

From the list above, select the TWO types of leader identified by Fiedler. (2 marks)

(Total: 4 marks)

2 **(a)** XYZ Company installed a computer system to handle its main accounting functions including accounts receivables, accounts payables and payroll. Management has a number of concerns about access to the system and are considering a number of controls to overcome those concerns.

The following are types of control they are considering:

A General control

B Information processing control

Required:

Classify the following as either A (General control) or B (Information processing control):

(i) Locking the computer room to prevent access to non-employees.

(ii) Limiting access to the payroll system by making it password protected.

(iii) Taking backup of data files each evening and holding backup copies off-premises.

(iv) Providing basic IT training to the entire staff to prevent errors in using the system.

Note: The total marks will be split equally between each part. **(2 marks)**

(b) The company has considerable cash collections on a regular basis. The cashier receives the cash, records it and then banks it at the end of each day. Since a single person is responsible for access to cash, the financial director is concerned that fraud and error may occur in cash handling and recording. He/she proposes use of appropriate internal controls to prevent any such errors or misappropriations.

The following are specific examples of internal controls used in business:

A Segregation of duties

B Induction and training

C Authorisation limit

D Internal audit

The following sentences contain gaps which specify the appropriate internal control which could be used to prevent fraud and errors.

Fraud and errors in handling cash can be prevented through 1 since no one individual could record and process a complete transaction.

Required:

(i) Select the correct internal control which appropriately fills gap 1 above; i.e. select A, B, C or D. **(1 mark)**

Even if such a measure were introduced, the possibility exists that staff could act together to perpetrate fraud and bypass this control. This can be prevented through 2 as it would ensure awareness of the heavy sanctions to be imposed in cases of dishonesty.

(ii) Select the correct internal control which appropriately fills gap 2 above; i.e. select A, B, C or D. **(1 mark)**

(Total: 4 marks)

3 There are a number of ways of developing staff on a one-to-one basis within organisations. Each has its own strengths and weaknesses and is appropriate in different work situations.

Examples of types of development include coaching, mentoring, counselling and appraising.

Required:

(a) For each type of development below, which work situation is most appropriate?

A An interview to help another person to identify and work through a problem.

B A longer term relationship in which a more experienced person encourages an individual's personal and career development.

C An approach whereby a trainee is put under the guidance of an experienced employee who shows the trainee how to perform tasks.

D An interview, the aim of which is to review performance and identify training and development needs.

(i) Coaching. Select ONE of A, B, C or D

(ii) Mentoring. Select ONE of A, B, C or D

(iii) Counselling. Select ONE of A, B, C or D

(iv) Appraising. Select ONE of A, B, C or D

Note: The total marks will be split equally between each part. (2 marks)

(b) An organisation uses mentoring as a form of one-to-one personal development.

A Determine remuneration

B Decide promotions

C Career and personal development

D Resolve a grievance

E Demonstrating how to perform

F Using experienced staff for training

G Providing a role model for an employee

Required:

Which TWO of the above are benefits of this approach? Select TWO from (A, B, C, D, E, F, G). (2 marks)

(Total: 4 marks)

4 Sport-4-Kidz is a charitable organisation that operates a sports centre in a large city.

The land on which the playing fields and facilities are located is held on behalf of the charity by Donna and Dietmar, the two trustees. Donna and Dietmar simply hold the land on behalf of Sport-4-Kidz and play no role in running the charity. They are rarely contacted by the management of the charity. However, they are the only people who are able to enter into contracts in relation to the land and its use.

Sport-4-Kidz is managed and operated by a management committee. The committee has decided on a major expansion of facilities by building a new sports hall. The committee has the power to legally bind the charity in all matters other than the land. Their decisions are overseen by the government charity regulator, which generally sanctions the charity's decisions except in relation to financial reporting.

The management committee is negotiating with four building companies.

The proposed expansion of the facilities has angered the local residents, many of whom are concerned about heavy building site traffic and the danger posed to their children. Many believe that the design of the new sports hall is ugly and insensitive. Three well-respected local politicians serve on the residents' committee.

(a) The following are types of stakeholder:

A Internal stakeholder

B External stakeholder

C Connected stakeholder

Required:

For each of the following, indicate whether they are internal, connected or external stakeholders.

(i) Donna and Dietmar. Select one of A, B or C

(ii) Members of the management committee. Select one of A, B or C

(iii) The four building companies. Select one of A, B or C

(iv) Local residents. Select one of A, B or C

Note: The total marks will be split equally between each part. **(2 marks)**

(b) Complete the following sentences about Sport-4-Kidz stakeholders, with reference to Mendelow's grid.

The local residents exert 1 and should be 2

(i) Select which ONE of the following fills Gap 1:

A high power, low interest

B high power, high interest

C low power, low interest

D low power, high interest

Write down A, B, C or D.

(ii) Select which ONE of the following fills Gap 2:

A treated as a key player

B kept satisfied

C kept informed

Write down A, B, or C.

The building companies exert 3 and should be 4

(iii) Select which ONE of the following fills Gap 3:

A high power, low interest

B high power, high interest

C low power, low interest

D low power, high interest

Write down A, B, C or D.

(iv) Select which ONE of the following fills Gap 4:

A treated as a key player

B kept satisfied

C kept informed

Write down A, B, or C.

Note: The total marks will be split equally between each part. **(2 marks)**

(Total: 4 marks)

5 Accounting bodies set out a code of ethics to establish ethical behaviour requirements for professional accountants.

(a) The following are qualities you might see in a professional at work:

Integrity **A**	Honesty **B**
Trustworthiness **C**	Expertise **D**
Professional behaviour **E**	Confidentiality **F**
Respectfulness **G**	Objectivity **H**

Required:

Select the FOUR boxes from (A–H) contain fundamental principles of ethical behaviour from the IFAC (IESBA) and ACCA codes of ethics. **(2 marks)**

(b) The following are desirable characteristics of professions and vocations:

A Acting in the public interest

B Highly skilled

C Ethical codes of conduct

D Highly valued services

E Training equipment

F Process of certification

G Presence of a governing organisation

H Qualification by examination

Required:

Select FOUR factors from the list above, which distinguish a profession from an occupation. (2 marks)

(Total: 4 marks)

6 **Company A** is an accountancy professional body which has a tall structure and a high level of centralisation. The span of control is very narrow. Subordinates have minimal latitude for self-determination or to influence decision-making and mainly concentrate on carrying out highly prescribed and defined roles.

Company B is a financial services company which gives a wide ranging role to its traders and promotes cultural values such as assertiveness, risk appetite, and a high degree of competition between employees. The employees are usually young and unmarried, and work and socialise together for long hours at a frenetic pace.

Company C is a research and development company where the business is divisionalised by product. Staff work very flexibly and often need to communicate laterally to achieve objectives through ad hoc projects and collaboration. There are no formal rules about reporting structures, or about set starting or finishing times. Staff are rewarded on the basis of creativity and innovation.

Company D is a family company which is highly controlled by the owners and the CEO is the main shareholder. There is a very low staff turnover, but employees are expected to be very loyal to the company and are often required to work long hours and carry out tasks outside their normal range of duties. Relationships between employees and managers are very informal and close and the rights of employees and their overall interests are strongly defended by the owners when challenged.

The following are dimensions used by Hofstede to classify types of organisational culture:

		1. High	**2. Low**
A	Power distance	A1	A2
B	Uncertainty avoidance	B1	B2
C	Individualism	C1	C2
D	Motivation towards achievement and success	D1	D2

Required:

(i) For Company A select which combination of dimensions apply from the grid above. (For example A1) (1 mark)

(ii) For Company B select which combination of dimensions apply from the grid above. (For example A1) (1 mark)

(iii) For Company C select which combination of dimensions apply from the grid above. (For example A1) (1 mark)

(iv) For Company D select which combination of dimensions apply from the grid above. (For example A1) (1 mark)

(Total: 4 marks)

Section 8

SPECIMEN EXAM ANSWERS

Section A

1 B

The IASB aims to promote consistency in corporate reporting by creating financial reporting standards to which major businesses are expected to adhere.

2 B

The leadership style that least acknowledges the contribution that subordinates have to make is autocratic.

3 B

Negotiation gives the best opportunity for the two sides in a conflict to converge their positions. The other options either involve backing down, forcing a position, potentially increasing conflict, or leaving the issue unresolved.

4 B

Mentors usually help staff on broader work related development, including orientation and induction. Coaches work on developing specific skills of the job itself, while counsellors work with people on a personal level, perhaps if they are having non-work related or emotional problems.

5 C

The board of directors are responsible for the well-being of a wide group of constituencies, including shareholders, but also employees and other internal, external and connected stakeholders.

6 A

Because of the particular circumstances of the scenario where someone is made redundant from an industry in decline where skills cannot be easily transferred, where re-training might take a long time or where work is not available in the short term within a reasonable geographic proximity, this is classed as structural unemployment.

7 B and C

Determining discounts requires understanding the financial impact on profits. The accounts department will track and analyse various costs, including distribution.

8 A and C

Detecting unusual patterns in key accounting ratios.

Predicting the probability of key risks materialising.

9 D

The ageing population trend is caused by a decreasing birth rate and a decreasing mortality rate.

10 B

The 'tell and listen' approach encourages input from the individual, promoting participation in the process by the appraisee.

11 B

The external auditor has to ensure that the financial statements of the organisation truly reflect the activities of the business in the relevant accounting period. This assessment should be independent and therefore free from subjectivity on the part of the management of the client organisation.

12 B

A self-review threat arises as the auditor (Amy) may be reviewing their own work or the work carried out by others in PFG Co.

13 A

An employee with a range of tasks or objectives to achieve and pressures to achieve them to set deadlines, should always prioritise tasks in accordance to business importance. Deciding on other criteria such as pressure applied by colleagues, whether someone is absent or not or simply because a task is urgent may damage wider business objectives.

14 D

A professional accountant acting in accordance with fundamental ethical principles is demonstrating objectivity when they give a complete and precise view, which by implication means that negative aspects should not be concealed or positive aspects accentuated.

15 C

IFAC has no legal powers against businesses, nor does it set financial reporting standards. It is an accounting association member body which promotes educational and ethical standards of behaviour amongst its member bodies, through a code of ethics and behaviour, but does not prescribe detailed rules on this.

16 B

An informal organisation is the social structure of the organization, as opposed to the formal structure of an organization.

17 C

Information on purchase costs of finished goods or raw materials is important in establishing the price of a product. In terms of the marketing mix, this information is most relevant to the price element as prices should be set at least to cover cost and give an acceptable level of profit.

18 B

An authorisation control affirms that a transaction is valid and typically takes the form of an approval by a higher level of management.

19 D

The key correctly matches the information required to the particular financial statement in which they are to be found.

20 A

The restaurant wishes to cater for the needs of more than one stakeholder group without seriously compromising the interests of any individual group. Therefore setting aside a special area for families with children while having an adults only section would achieve this.

21 B

Data protection legislation is formulated to protect the interests of data subjects who are private individuals. Not all data is regulated.

22 A

A transaction processing system enables all sales and purchase transactions to be recorded by volume and category.

23 B

B is correct because customers and suppliers deal closely on a transactional basis with the organisation, but are not internal stakeholders like managers and executive directors.

24 A

Where price inflation is high the value of money reduces consistently over time. Those who owe money (debtors) therefore pay back less capital in real terms, and interest rates seldom adjust adequately to compensate for this.

25 A

Role playing exercises are most effectively used for skills development, including sales training.

26 B

The Blake and Mouton managerial grid enables leadership styles to be categorised on a nine point scale with reference to concern for production and concern for people. Renata is therefore highly concerned with the task and much less interested in her team as individuals.

27 B

The implementation of a budgetary control system would be the responsibility of the financial controller in many organisations. The internal auditor is not responsible for implementing systems, but is involved in monitoring the effectiveness of these systems.

28 C

The external auditor is responsible for ensuring that financial reports portray a true and fair view and comply with legal disclosure requirements. External auditors are not responsible for ensuring that systems exist to prevent fraud.

29 A

Integrity is about honesty and applying morality to business and professional behaviour. A person acting with integrity should not be corruptible. Neutrality in the making of business decisions does not indicate morality nor does producing accurate work, which is more about professional competence.

30 B

Only shareholders have voting power related to the number of shares that they own. Members of a co-operative organisation can vote but will only have one vote. Co-operatives may be owned by members, but ownership stakes cannot be exchanged between members unless the members belong to limited companies.

31 B

Synergy refers to the process that occurs when a group, by acting together, achieves an outcome that is superior to what would be achieved by any simple pooling of individual member efforts, often summarised by the phrases 'the whole is greater than the sum of the parts' or '2 + 2 = 5.'

32 D

Blockchain information does NOT require a greater need for the auditing of transactions.

33 B

The task culture is appropriate where organisations can accommodate the flexibility required to adjust management and team structures to address the tasks that must be fulfilled. This is very common in large consultancy firms.

34 D

Oligopoly markets are markets dominated by a small number of suppliers, who have high levels of influence within their market.

35 C

According to Herzberg, motivators, such as recognition, achievement and responsibility make workers more productive, creative and committed.

36 C

Corporate governance codes are designed to ensure that companies operate in a way that is ethical, transparent and accountable.

37 D

The primary aim of a public oversight board is to eliminate or minimise any actual or potential breaches of legislative requirements and to ensure compliance with regulations applicable to organisations within their terms of reference.

38 B

Scientific management principles consider the ways in which the factors of production (land, labour, capital and the entrepreneurial function) can be combined to maximise efficiency in production. The founding principles are based on the work of Frederick Winslow Taylor. The reorganisation of the call centre follows these principles.

39 A

A personal development planning is a structured framework you can use to become aware of skills you have, identify and develop skills you need and work out what you want to achieve and how to achieve it.

40 A

The four Ps are Product, Price, Promotion and Place.

41 B

Decentralisation devolves authority to lower levels and gives more autonomy to individuals and teams. Decentralisation on the other hand increases risk as there is less control over individual and group behaviour and decision-making. Allowing more freedom to act independently leads to less consistency across the organisation.

42 A

Compliance with legal requirements may not eliminate unethical behaviour. The issues of concern to those who complain may not be fully representative of issues of concern to customers in general. Other companies in the sector may not be concerned about ethical behaviour.

43 C

Using SWOT analysis, the way to conduct this analysis would be for the individual to consider their own strengths and weaknesses and how they could affect the impression given to others. The other options are external factors to the individual so would not directly affect the opinion that others would have of that individual.

44 B

As new members are about to join the group, essentially the group is reforming which is the start of a new group development process. The other options are all later stages in group development as identified by Tuckman.

45 A

Teeming and lading involves the theft of cash and is a type of fraud that is carried out by manipulating transactions. There would be most potential for this fraud within the sales department where cash may be received and remitted.

46 B

The demand curve of a company in a perfect market is horizontal, because they can sell as much as they want at a given market price and nothing at all at a price set higher than the prevailing market price.

Section B

1 **(a)** (i) D

(ii) B

(iii) A

(iv) C

Rationale: The individual writers given in the key are associated with the relevant management theory

(b) A and B

2 **(a)** (i) A

(ii) A

(iii) A

(iv) B

(b) (i) A

(ii) B

3 **(a)** (i) C

(ii) B

(iii) A

(iv) D

(b) C and G

4 **(a)** (i) C

(ii) A

(iii) C

(iv) B

(b) (i) B

(ii) A

(iii) D

(iv) C

5 **(a)** A, E, F, H

(b) A, C, F, G

6 (i) A1

(ii) D1

(iii) B2

(iv) C2